Communicating Identities

Communicating Identities is a book for language teachers who wish to focus on the topic of identity in the context of their classroom teaching. The work provides an accessible introduction to research and theory on language learner and language teacher identity. It provides a set of interactive, practical activities for use in language classrooms in which students explore and communicate about aspects of their identities. The communicative activities concern the various facets of the students' own identities and are practical resources that teachers can draw on to structure and guide their students' exploration of their identities. All the activities include a follow-on teacher reflection in which teachers explore aspects of their own identity in relation to the learner identities explored in the activities. The book also introduces teachers to practical steps in doing exploratory action research so that they can investigate identity systematically in their own classrooms.

Gary Barkhuizen is a professor of applied linguistics at the University of Auckland, New Zealand. His teaching and research interests are in the areas of language teacher education, teacher and learner identity, study abroad, and narrative inquiry. He is editor of *Reflections on Language Teacher Identity Research* (Routledge, 2017) and *Qualitative Research Topics in Language Teacher Education* (Routledge, 2019).

Pat Strauss is an associate professor at Auckland University of Technology, New Zealand. Her teaching and research interests include academic writing, student and teacher identity, language teacher education, and English for research and publication purposes.

Research and Resources in Language Teaching

Series Editors: Anne Burns, University of New South Wales, Australia, and Jill Hadfield, Unitec Institute of Technology, New Zealand

Research and Resources in Language Teaching is a groundbreaking series that aims to integrate the latest research in language teaching and learning with innovative classroom practice. Books in the series offer accessible accounts of current research on a particular topic, linked to a wide range of practical and immediately usable classroom activities.

Digital Literacies
Gavin Dudeney, Nicky Hockly, and Mark Pegrum

Motivating Learning
Zoltán Dörnyei and Jill Hadfield

Active Listening
Michael Rost and J. J. Wilson

Reflective Dialogue
Advising in Language Learning
Satoko Kato and Jo Mynard

Teacher Development Over Time
Practical Activities for Language Teachers
Tessa Woodward, Kathleen Graves, and Donald Freeman

Communicating Identities
Gary Barkhuizen and Pat Strauss

For more information about this series, please visit: www.routledge.com/Research-and-Resources-in-Language-Teaching/book-series/PEARRLT

Communicating Identities

Gary Barkhuizen and Pat Strauss

NEW YORK AND LONDON

First published 2020
by Routledge
52 Vanderbilt Avenue, New York, NY 10017

and by Routledge
2 Park Square, Milton Park, Abingdon, Oxon, OX14 4RN

Routledge is an imprint of the Taylor & Francis Group, an informa business

© 2020 Taylor & Francis

The right of Gary Barkhuizen and Pat Strauss to be identified as authors of this work has been asserted by them in accordance with sections 77 and 78 of the Copyright, Designs and Patents Act 1988.

All rights reserved. No part of this book may be reprinted or reproduced or utilised in any form or by any electronic, mechanical, or other means, now known or hereafter invented, including photocopying and recording, or in any information storage or retrieval system, without permission in writing from the publishers.

Trademark notice: Product or corporate names may be trademarks or registered trademarks, and are used only for identification and explanation without intent to infringe.

Library of Congress Cataloging-in-Publication Data
Names: Barkhuizen, Gary Patrick, author. | Strauss, Pat, author.
Title: Communicating identities / Gary Barkhuizen & Pat Strauss.
Description: New York : Routledge, 2020. | Series: Research and resources in language teaching | Includes bibliographical references and index.
Identifiers: LCCN 2019047491 (print) | LCCN 2019047492 (ebook) |
    ISBN 9781138295513 (hardback) | ISBN 9781138295520 (paperback) |
    ISBN 9781315100630 (ebook)
Subjects: LCSH: Language and languages—Study and teaching—Foreign
    speakers. | Second language acquisition. | Minority students—Education. |
    Language and education. | Multicultural education.
Classification: LCC P118.2 .B365 2020 (print) | LCC P118.2 (ebook) |
    DDC 418.0071—dc23
LC record available at https://lccn.loc.gov/2019047491
LC ebook record available at https://lccn.loc.gov/2019047492

ISBN: 978-1-138-29551-3 (hbk)
ISBN: 978-1-138-29552-0 (pbk)
ISBN: 978-1-315-10063-0 (ebk)

Typeset in Helvetica
by Apex CoVantage, LLC

To Johann and to Derek
For always communicating their identities

Contents

Acknowledgements		*x*
1	**From Research to Implications**	**1**
	A. Introduction	1
	B. Organization of Part 1	3
	C. Starting With the Big Issues	3
	D. Conceptualizing Language Learner Identity	7
	E. Conceptualizing Language Teacher Identity	16
	F. Implications of Identity Research for Application	21
	G. Looking Ahead: Communicating Identities	25
2	**From Implications to Application**	**26**
	A. Introduction	26
	B. Reflexing Identities	30
	Activity 1: This Is (Not) Like Me	33
	Activity 2: Celebrating Birthdays	35
	Activity 3: What Makes Me Me?	38
	Activity 4: Tweeting	42
	Activity 5: Memories and Smells	46
	Activity 6: Maps of the World	49
	Activity 7: Using Our Brains!	53
	Activity 8: The Genders of Objects	58
	Activity 9: Food and Identity	61
	Activity 10: Author Presence	66
	Activity 11: Chickens in Cages	70
	Activity 12: My Ideal Holiday	75
	C. Projecting Identities	79
	Activity 13: Introducing Ourselves	82
	Activity 14: What's in a Name?	86

Contents

	Activity 15: Gay Men Playing Rugby	90
	Activity 16: Relationships and Age	93
	Activity 17: The Clothes We Wear	95
	Activity 18: Why Is Facebook So Popular?	98
	Activity 19: Idiomatic Language	103
	Activity 20: Make Your Own Cartoon	106
	Activity 21: There's a Little Bit of Good in Everyone	111
	Activity 22: Proverbs and You	114
	Activity 23: Justifying Your Opinion	119
	Activity 24: Pictures at an Exhibition	122
D.	Recognizing Identities	125
	Activity 25: A Good Friend	128
	Activity 26: Who Are These Women?	131
	Activity 27: Film Critic	134
	Activity 28: Identity Theft	138
	Activity 29: Teacher Roles	141
	Activity 30: Gendered Identities in Occupations	145
	Activity 31: Stereotyping	148
	Activity 32: Questioning National Identities	151
	Activity 33: Designing a Questionnaire	156
	Activity 34: Writing a Report	160
	Activity 35: No Laughing Matter	165
	Activity 36: The Language of Ads	169
E.	Imagining Identities	173
	Activity 37: What Kind of Wild Animal?	175
	Activity 38: Me Flying High	178
	Activity 39: My Dream Room	182
	Activity 40: Names for (Online) Gamers	185
	Activity 41: The Aliens Have Landed	189
	Activity 42: Speaking English Tomorrow	192
	Activity 43: Identity Quotes	195
	Activity 44: Different Perspectives	199
	Activity 45: What Makes Them Them?	202

Activity 46: Social Justice and Advertising 205
Activity 47: Consumer Identity 208
Activity 48: Transport of the Future 213

3 From Application to Implementation **219**

A. Introduction 219
B. Organization of Part 3 220
C. Characteristics of the Curriculum 220
D. Planning Activities 223
E. Implementing Activities in the Classroom 225
F. What Should We Do After the Activities? 234

4 From Implementation to Research **237**

A. Introduction 237
B. Organization of Part 4 238
C. What Is Exploratory Action Research? 238
D. Selecting Topics to Explore 242
E. Gathering Information 248
F. Narrative Inquiry 252
G. Making Sense of the Information Gathered 254
H. Sharing Your Findings 263
I. Conclusion 265

References 266
Index 270

Acknowledgements

The authors are grateful to Helen Basturkmen for her contribution to conceptualizing the book and for designing parts of a number of the activities. We thank also series editors Anne Burns and Jill Hadfield for their support and feedback during the writing and revising process.

Part 1

From Research to Implications

A. Introduction

For many years now we have known that *learning* a language is much more than acquiring a set of linguistic skills and related competencies that enable learners to use the language appropriately in particular contexts. We also now know that language *teaching* is much more than simply passing on these skills and competencies to learners. In other words, learners are not empty vessels to be filled, and teachers are not merely technicians programed to do the filling. By learning a language, people change who they are. Language learners construct new identities as they learn. Bonny Norton (1995, 2013) has been telling us for years that investing in a language is also investing in identity.

This book is about the process of investing in identity in the language classroom, in interaction with other learners and with language teachers. Language learning takes place when people interact with others in language learning contexts. In other words, both language learning and identity construction are social processes in which learners communicate with social partners such as teachers and other learners. As Tracy and Robles (2013) say, "The identities a person brings to an interaction influence how that person communicates. At the same time, the specific discursive practices a person chooses will shape who he or she is taken to be, and who the partner is taken to be" (pp. 25–26).

The activities in this book all involve learners interacting in communicative activities in the classroom. The design of the activities means that learners engage with other learners and with the teacher and at the same time get the opportunity to reflect independently and in collaboration with others on various dimensions of identity. And the identities they explore include their own, as well as those of others in the classroom, friends and family, and people well beyond the confines of their familiar institutional and community spaces.

Research on identity and its connection to language learning reveals a relationship that has become increasingly more complex and broad in scope over recent years. One reason is that diverse and sometimes competing theoretical and methodological perspectives have produced different understandings of the processes of identity construction and what identity means for learners and learning. Another reason has to do with broader issues and developments in the field of language education, as well as in other disciplines and in the world generally, such as globalization.

In envisaging a research agenda for the future of identity in language learning and teaching, Peter De Costa and Bonny Norton (2016) draw attention to a number of current issues and developments that illustrate the diversity and scope in the field. These will inevitably find their way into language classroom activities that have as their goal *communicating identities*. We introduce them early in the book to stress the point that identity in language learning and teaching encompasses a wide range of current matters increasingly relevant to what happens with people in language classrooms and well beyond.

Although this research is often quick to suggest that identity should explicitly be a focus in the language classroom by, for example, incorporating identity-related activities into communicative lessons, it is by no means easy to do. And it is even more challenging to design an entirely identity-oriented curriculum for a class of learners over time. What identity issues or topics related to identity do we include in the activities? What shape do identity-oriented lessons take? Is an identity-focused curriculum even feasible? We believe it is, and so this book takes up the challenge. We do so by first reviewing relevant research and considering its implications in Part 1. Then in Part 2 we transform the research outcomes into practical classroom activities. Part 3 suggests ways in which the activities could be integrated into curricula in different teaching contexts, and Part 4 returns to research, this time in the form of suggestions for identity-related teacher research, particularly exploratory action research and narrative inquiry.

B. Organization of Part 1

In Section C, we briefly introduce seven developments from De Costa and Norton's (2016, pp. 587–591) research agenda and then come back to them during the discussion that follows later in Part 1. They will also be evident throughout the activities that make up Part 2 of the book.

We then turn in Section D to Norton's (2013) conceptualization of language learner identity. In this section we break down her poststructuralist description of identity into sub-sections, each representing themes that have been extensively covered by identity researchers over the past couple of decades. As we explain later in Part 1, *teacher identity* is also central to understanding language learning and teaching. In Section E we thus explore teacher identity further by analyzing Barkhuizen's (2017) conceptualization of language teacher identity, making comparisons with learner identity along the way.

Both these conceptualizations and the big issues that start this part of the book in the next section generate a number of implications. We articulate these in the form of four facets of identity, which are described in the final section of Part 1.

C. Starting With the Big Issues

In this section we briefly discuss seven relevant developments from De Costa and Norton's (2016) research agenda for identity in language learning and teaching.

1. Globalization

   - involves blending and intersecting movements of people
   - leads to increasing multilingualism in schools and society
   - is characterized by heightened individualism rather than communities sharing and working together, as well as competition amongst people and between institutions

From Research to Implications

Identity is not just about sitting in a monolingual classroom and working through textbook activities prescribed by the teacher. Language classrooms are diverse socio-political spaces that are influenced by powerful phenomena and ideologies outside in the world. Language learners and their teachers—what they do and who they are—are very much linked to these external conditions.

2. Investment

- refers to learners' commitment and intentional choices and desires
- relates to issues of identity and the futures they imagine for themselves
- lies at the intersection of identity, capital (e.g., economic, social status, language proficiency), and ideology

When learners invest in language learning, they expect some sort of yield. They will acquire language, but they will also acquire a wider range of capital, including social and economic capital. Of course, this means investing in their identities as well. Learning a language changes who they are, and this has consequences for their relationships with other people, including their relations of power.

Further Reading

Norton, B. (2015). Identity, investment, and faces of English internationally. *Chinese Journal of Applied Linguistics*, *38*(4), 375–391.

Sample Study

Sung, C. C. M. (2019). Investments and identities across contexts: A case study of a Hong Kong undergraduate student's L2 learning experiences. *Journal of Language, Identity and Education*, *18*(3), 190–203.

---

3. Intersectionality

- means social identity categories that intersect or overlap such as ethnicity, race, gender, religion, and social class
- occurs within contexts of globalization and its structures of inequality (see earlier)

4

From Research to Implications

Social identities are not easily categorized as one type or another. This is because we have multiple identities, and they are always changing. They are dynamic and change according to the social interactions in which speakers participate. A language learner's racial and religious identities, for example, may intersect and become more foregrounded when they interact with speakers of a dominant language and culture.

4. Social theory across disciplines

- provides multiple perspectives of the self, including psychological and complexity perspectives
- theorizes agency not as a feature of the learner but as performed and constituted in social interaction with others
- relates identity to, for example, ideology, moral stance, and emotion

The quest for deeper understandings of identity in language learning has recently turned transdisciplinary. Meaningful insights are being sought, both theoretically and methodologically, among different fields of study such as developmental psychology, economics, and anthropology.

5. Digital literacy

- comprises multiple (digital) literacies and their relationship to language education and identity
- expands the range of identities available to language learners

Technology and other digital resources (e.g., social media) give learners access to a wider range of potential literacies with which to shape and transform their identities and to interpret those of others. However, in poorly resourced communities where digital technologies (and even electricity) are not readily available, digital and multimodal literacies research and pedagogy are severely limited.

6. Scales

- include timescales, from short periods of time to learners' longer personal and language learning histories

From Research to Implications

- involve development of identities over scales of space—movement across physical and social spaces

Identity negotiation and construction take place within three interrelated scales that expand outward. The micro level of social activity includes interpersonal interactions, such as those we see in classrooms between teachers and learners. The meso or middle level includes broader institutional and community spaces, and the broadest macro level includes ideological structures such as belief systems and political and economic values (Douglas Fir Group, 2016). Therefore, language learning and teaching activities and learner identities are interconnected with contexts well beyond those of classrooms (e.g., schools; local communities; city councils; geographical regions; state and national governments; regional and global political movements, such as Brexit and right-wing extremism, respectively).

7. Teacher identities

- are constantly reforming in the globalized world
- are enacted in language classrooms in interaction with language learners
- are at the intersection of teachers' language learning, teacher education, and teaching practice

Language teachers' personal and professional identities are constructed, performed, contested, and valued in interaction with their learners in classrooms and with colleagues in their institutions. Their identities are not only who they are but also what they do—their practice. In any classroom, at any time, the language *teacher's* identities and the many language *learners'* identities are all at play.

That is why in this book, the communicative activities, designed for language learning through the exploration of identity-related topics, all include an opportunity for the teacher (or teacher educator) to reflect on their own identity in relation to the topic of that particular activity. In the next two sections we explore conceptualization of identity in more detail. The first examines language *learner* identity, drawing on Bonny Norton's influential work that has inspired teachers and researchers for many

6

years. The section after that considers language *teacher* identity and discusses a conceptualization put together by Gary Barkhuizen (2017) based on the ideas and experiences of numerous scholars in the field. Although this latter conceptualization concerns teacher identity, it applies very much to learners as well.

D. Conceptualizing Language Learner Identity

Having provided a broad overview of issues and developments in identity research in language learning and teaching, we now focus more specifically on what identity means. Theoretical perspectives on language learner identity have changed over time, reflecting shifting philosophical trends in the social and human sciences, as we have seen in the opening paragraphs above. Also, researchers working in and within different disciplines (e.g., education, second language acquisition, psychology) have varying ideas about how identity might be conceptualized in their work. In spite of the challenges of coming up with a definition of identity, Norton (2013, p. 45) offers a very clear and useful description of recent thinking about identity. Seven phrases in this description have been italicized and numbered, and these are discussed after the extract.

I use the term identity to reference how a person understands his or her *relationship to the world*,[1] how that relationship is *constructed across time and space*,[2] and how the person understands *possibilities for the future*.[3] I argue that SLA [second language acquisition] theory needs to develop a conception of identity that is understood with reference to larger, and frequently *inequitable, social structures*[4] which are reproduced in *day-to-day social interaction*.[5] In taking this position, I foreground the role of *language as constitutive of and constituted by*[6] a language learner's identity. . . . It is through language that a person negotiates a sense of self within and across different sites at

From Research to Implications

> different points in time, and it is through language that a person
> gains access to—or is denied access to—powerful social networks
> that *give learners the opportunity to speak.*[7]

1. Relationship to the World

Identities are constructed within social relationships between people—
people, with attitudes, beliefs, expectations, feelings, and assumptions
in local communities (e.g., face-to-face interactions in classrooms) and
in global communities (e.g., on the internet).

We relate not only to *people* in the world, however, but also to
social structures which take the form of institutions, policies, cultural
practices, laws, and so on. In educational contexts, examples at a
micro level include the curriculum and teachers' pedagogical practices
in classrooms. At the macro level, education policies, language policies
and assessment regimes make up these structures.

How people understand their relationship to these people and
structures shapes their identities. This perspective is quite different
from perspectives on identity that tend to emphasize the biological
make-up of people, for example, their sex and skin color, or other 'static'
classifications, such as country of birth and social group membership
(national, ethnic, and religious, for example), where both they and all
members of the group then become defined in a delimited, rigid way,
with external definitions imposed upon them.

This latter perspective on identity is usually referred to as *essentialism*,
that is, "the position that the attributes and behavior of socially defined
groups can be determined and explained by reference to cultural and/
or biological characteristics believed to be inherent to the groups"
(Bucholtz, 2003, p. 400).

Language learners' worlds of people and social structures include
their classrooms and schools or other institutions, and in these spaces
they interact with other learners and teachers. However, their social

interactions extend well beyond the classroom walls on broader scales, for example, via online digital spaces, in their families, in the community, and possibly even in transnational contexts. Learners negotiate and shape their identities (i.e., they are always changing) as they constantly try to understand who they are in relation to their micro and macro worlds.

2. Constructed Across Time and Space

In contrast to essentialism, the idea that identity is constructed across time and space implies that it is fluid and changeable. People's identities are constructed in relationship to the world at different times (including their histories and imagined futures) and in different spaces (both real and imagined, including physical locations and social spaces).

Once again, the times and places can be experienced at both micro and macro levels. For instance, time can be quite a long period, such as one's entire life span, or it can be only a short moment, such as an informal conversation lasting a few seconds. Identities also change in spaces that are micro (e.g., a face-to-face discussion between two people in a coffee shop) and macro (e.g., participating in an international webinar with hundreds of participants).

This situation represents a complex, ongoing (re)arranging of the dimensions of time and space—which is the world that people interconnect with when constructing their identity, or more accurately *identities*, since within these dynamic temporal and spatial arrangements, people inevitably have multiple identities. A language teacher, for example, may also be a mother, an immigrant, and a community leader. Pre-immigration she would have experienced identities that might not be evident now in her post-immigration life.

These ideas about identity reflect a *poststructuralist* perspective, that is, moving beyond the confines of constant social structures and essentialist understandings of identity. Because of this, some researchers prefer the term *subject positions* to identities; we are always positioning ourselves, as subjects, in our relationships with others and

From Research to Implications

the world. There is no standing still. At the same time, however, Norton (1997) explains that we are "both subject of and subject to" (p. 411) these relationships, meaning that sometimes rather than being the agent of our positioning, we are positioned by our relationships.

The same, of course, applies to language learners. Learners are positioned by others, including their teachers, other learners, and members of the wider society, and this positioning might not always be beneficial to them or acceptable to them. At the same time, they strive, because of their desires and through the social interactions they engage in, to make a place for themselves in their worlds—in classrooms and outside. As we know, this is not always easy.

3. Possibilities for the Future

How people imagine themselves in the future relates very much to how they understand who they are in the present. For language learners, this has implications not only for how they make sense of who they are as language learners but also for how they go about their learning. As Kanno and Norton (2003) say, "what has not yet happened in the future can be a reason and motivation for what learners do in the present" (p. 248).

Immigrant language learners who express a desire for a better life in a new country, for example, often report that it is necessary to be a successful learner of the dominant language of that country. They argue that this will enable them to secure employment, improve their education, and interact productively with others in their communities. In other words, they imagine themselves as successful, happy members of their imagined communities. It is for reasons such as these that learners enroll in language classes and *invest* in language learning.

Through investing in an additional language (particularly the language which has value in a community, such as the dominant language in an immigrant context), learners hope to acquire certain resources that have value for them. These include those that are *symbolic*, such as the language itself, education, and friendship, and those that are *material*, such as goods, money, and property.

And once these resources have been acquired (and even while they are being acquired), learners increase their value as members of society, that is, they increase their cultural and social capital. Because this situation has obvious implications for the learner's identity, it is reasonable to conclude that an investment in language learning is also an investment in the learner's own identity (see Darvin & Norton, 2015).

Further Reading

Pavlenko, A., & Norton, B. (2007). Imagined communities, identity, and English language learning. In J. Cummins & C. Davison (Eds.), *International handbook of English language teaching* (pp. 669–680). Boston, MA: Springer.

Sample Study

Yim, S. Y. (2016). EFL young learners: Their imagined communities and language learning. *English Language Teaching Journal*, *70*(1), 57–65.

---

4. Inequitable, Social Structures

To sum up so far, identities are constructed in relationships with people and social structures in varying scales of contexts, from micro to macro levels. These social structures are frequently inequitable; that is, there are people and social structures that have more value or power than others. Those who find themselves in marginalized positions are denied access to the very resources they need or desire to become successful, legitimate, valued members of society. Of course, for those who have power and who want to keep it, this is an ideal situation. They want to maintain the status quo and so do not want any inequitable relations of power to be revealed or challenged.

The ideologies underlying their relative positions are a way to legitimize the existing social relations and differences of power. In other words, it seems right and natural that the unequal relationships between people are the way they are. The way these social structures and relationships are maintained and perceived vary considerably in different sociocultural and geopolitical contexts. There is no one way of addressing the inequity pedagogically, therefore. Some teachers and schools are content to leave things the way they are, and for others it does not even cross their minds that they should be transforming their practices in any way. Generally, however, a *critical* pedagogical approach would aim to unravel and expose these hidden relations of power. The way teachers teach and learners learn, and the types of materials and assessments teachers select, for example, would lead to the uncovering, understanding, and potential transformation of the unequal conditions in which language education takes place. The aim of doing so is for teachers and learners to explore their identity options both inside and outside the classroom and to negotiate positions where access to desired resources and capital (e.g., economic, social) is achieved.

Taken from a scales perspective (micro, meso, macro) as described, negotiation could take place even on a very small level, such as between learners during one classroom lesson, or on a larger scale between learners and members of their community outside the classroom. As Pavlenko and Blackledge (2004) say, negotiation "may take place between individuals, between majority and minority groups, and, most importantly, between institutions and those they are supposed to serve" (p. 3). Inequality means that some people, groups, and institutions have more power than others, but those with less power do not always accept the positions they find themselves in. This signals the often conflictual nature of identity negotiation in situations in which unequal power relations are evident.

5. Day-to-Day Social Interaction

As we have already said, researchers currently view identity as something people do—something we construct during discourse.

From Research to Implications

In other words, identity is constructed in interaction with others and involves the use of language and other semiotic, or meaning-making, means such as gestures, facial expressions, and material objects in particular social contexts. According to Gee (1990, p. xix), discourses are "ways of behaving, interacting, valuing, thinking, believing, speaking, and often reading and writing that are accepted as instantiations of particular roles by specific groups of people."

Gee's well-known definition presents a very broad understanding of discourses. At the risk of oversimplifying its meaning, the definition describes discourses as ways of knowing what to do in particular contexts with particular people and how to interact (through all semiotic means) with those people in those contexts—both micro (immediate) and macro (broader sociocultural-political) contexts.

For example, it is possible to identify a *language teaching and learning* discourse. Imagine being at a language teacher conference or workshop. Participants will hear and talk about issues to do quite specifically with language teaching, such as pedagogical practices, policy implementation, course structures, classroom materials, and second language acquisition theory and research; they will view visual presentations about these topics; they will read handouts; there will be informal discussion over morning tea; there may also be book exhibits and poster displays. These visual and aural contributions will be consumed by participants who will be familiar with the vocabulary, beliefs, pictures, and emotions they encounter or generate themselves. However, these same conference participants may struggle to engage effectively and confidently in a workshop for plumbers, where a *plumbing* discourse would be quite unfamiliar to them.

Norton (2013) makes the point in her definition that the inequitable social structures that people intersect with (see previous section) are reproduced in day-to-day discursive interaction; that is, they are embedded in the interaction and therefore have an influence on the trajectory and identity outcomes of the interaction. It is clear, therefore, that when we talk about identity, we mean *doing* identity (it is relational)

13

rather than *being* or *having* an identity (i.e., it is not interior and fixed, or something we possess). A language learner, for example, is being a language learner (i.e., performs a language learner identity) when he or she is participating in a communicative task during a language lesson. 'Language learner' is not an identity they inherently possess and carry around with them all the time in all contexts.

Beauchamp and Thomas (2009) comment on the language used in the identity literature to describe this process of identification—the shaping or construction of identities. They identify a number of 'action' words that reflect the dynamic, active nature of the process, including developing, constructing, forming, negotiating, identity-making, creating, shaping, and building. Whatever term, the process it describes clearly indicates an *inter*-action which occurs when people discursively engage with one other.

6. Language as Constitutive of and Constituted By

Norton's (2013) definition of identity emphasizes very forcefully the role that language plays in identity construction. This relationship, of course, is central to the rationale for this book—it is what underlies all the activities and prompts ideas for an identity-oriented curriculum and for further research in identity in language learning and teaching.

Language is central in understanding the relationship between individuals and the social world. Language connects people to the social, and it is through language that people negotiate and construct their identities and understand who they are. Ivanič (2006) says that "language is a means of identification" (p. 22). She distinguishes three ways in which language can contribute to the construction of identity: (1) by *address*; the way we are talked to by others; (2) by *attribution*; the way we are talked about by others, and (3) by *affiliation*; the way we talk like others. The activities in Part 2 include many examples of these three types of identification.

Bourdieu (1977), a French sociologist, says that "language is worth what those who speak it are worth" (p. 652). What he means is that who we are (our identities) is linked to the languages we know and use. Some languages (or varieties of languages) are perceived to be 'worth' more than others because of the social prestige they have, and different values are attached to speakers of languages who are more or less proficient in them. Languages that are worth more have more power, and people who are worth more have more power. But as the previous sections have shown, languages and people cannot in themselves have power; it is in interactions between people and between people and institutions where relations of power become evident and where the negotiation of identities takes place.

Language learners always find themselves at the intersection of languages coming into contact—their own (which may be more than one), the languages of other learners, and the language they are learning. When Norton (2013) says language is constitutive of and constituted by a language learner's identity she means that learners negotiate their way through the various meanings and values attached to the different languages they encounter and use in social interaction, including classroom learning activities, and in the process negotiate a sense of who they are—their identity.

7. Give Learners the Opportunity to Speak

Language gives individuals access to people and communities that afford them opportunities to acquire the symbolic (including language) and material resources that they desire. But to achieve these goals it is necessary that they have access, either through their own agency or through being offered opportunities by the people and social networks they engage with.

Those in powerful positions, as already noted, sometimes deny those in less powerful positions (e.g., language learners, migrants, refugees) such opportunities. For language learners, this means being denied opportunities to use and practice the language they are learning. And as in a vicious circle, not learning the language means not attaining the desired resources.

From Research to Implications

In language classrooms, it is the responsibility of the teacher to provide practice opportunities to their learners. In addition, pedagogy and learning cannot be effective unless teachers engage with the identities of their learners. They need to create opportunities for learners to explore their changing identities and to imagine possible future identities in relation to what and how they learn (i.e., to enable learners to identify with their language learning). All the activities in Part 2 of this book aim to mediate such learning.

E. Conceptualizing Language Teacher Identity

As with language learners, knowing about teachers and 'who they are' — their identities — is necessary for our understanding of what is going on in schools and classrooms. With regard to language teachers, Varghese, Morgan, Johnston, and Johnson (2005, p. 22) say:

> In order to understand language teaching and learning we need to understand teachers; and in order to understand teachers, we need to have a clearer sense of who they are: the professional, cultural, political, and individual identities which they claim or which are assigned to them.

Teachers are thinking and feeling human beings who make professional decisions while working in particular sociocultural, political contexts. In the process they construct identities for themselves and are also assigned identities by others in those contexts and by their institutions.

The important message here is that if we want to understand language teaching and learning, we need to know about teachers' identities — what they are, how they are negotiated and constructed, and how they relate to both their teaching, and more important, their learners and *their* learning.

A concluding theme in much recent research on language teacher identity is that it is necessary for teachers themselves to be aware of

From Research to Implications

their own identities and how they relate to their practices. The implication of this research, therefore, is that teacher education and professional development programs (and teachers' own self-reflective practices) should offer opportunities for teachers to systematically examine their working lives to better understand 'who they are'. When teachers know who they are they are better able to connect with their learners in the classroom—and with colleagues, and administrators, and policies, and communities. They make more sense of the curriculum and how appropriate it is for their learners, they more accurately understand their learners' needs and desires, and they construct opportunities for their learners to practice listening, speaking, reading and writing. Teachers play a centrally important role in the way such learning opportunities are made available in the classroom for their learners. They do this through their pedagogical decisions and their practices, including those that make materials and activities available to their learners.

How then is *language teacher identity* conceptualized? Like language *learner* identity, this is not an easy question to answer as there are multiple theoretical perspectives on the topic. In a recent edited book on language teacher identity, the editor (Barkhuizen, 2017) thematically analyzed all the chapters, in which the authors reflected on their perceptions of teacher identity in their area of scholarly expertise, and produced a composite conceptualization of language teacher identity—a broad 'definition' that aimed to capture the various theoretical perspectives on language teacher identity drawn from the ideas in the chapters and which is arguably applicable beyond the scope of the book as well.

In many ways, the conceptualization is also applicable to language *learner* identity. For example, it starts by making reference to cognitive and social aspects of identity. Teacher identities are cognitive in that teachers constantly strive to understand themselves; reflexively, they work towards trying to make sense of who they are and who they desire or fear to be. Further, teacher identities are cognitive because they concern teachers' beliefs and theories about language teaching, and they relate to their content and pedagogical knowledge. All of

From Research to Implications

this applies to learners, too—learners have beliefs about language and language learning, and their identities relate to their knowledge of language.

Language teacher identities are also obviously social. They are enacted, constructed, negotiated, and projected with others—their language learners, teacher colleagues, administrators, and policy makers—within both local (e.g., in the classroom, in the staffroom, and in meeting places) and more global contexts (e.g., the language teaching profession). Gee (2000) supports this social view. He says identity is "being recognized as a certain 'kind of person', in a given context" (p. 99). Our identity is partly how other people see us, but it is also how we see ourselves, our own understanding of who we are. This is the same, of course, for language learners.

The composite conceptualization (Barkhuizen, 2017, p. 4) is followed by a brief discussion of some of its components, focusing specifically on teacher identity. But in reading the discussion (and the conceptualization), keep in mind how it may apply to the identity of language learners as well.

Language teacher identities (LTIs) are cognitive, social, emotional, ideological, and historical—they are both inside the teacher and outside in the social, material, and technological world. LTIs are being and doing, feeling and imagining, and storying. They are struggle and harmony: they are contested and resisted, by self and others, and they are also accepted, acknowledged, and valued, by self and others. They are core and peripheral, personal, and professional; they are dynamic, multiple, and hybrid; and they are foregrounded and backgrounded. And LTIs change, in the short term and over time—discursively in social interaction with teacher educators, learners, teachers, administrators, and the wider community and in material interaction with spaces, places, and objects in classrooms, institutions, and online.

The main thrust of the conceptualization is what has already been mentioned concerning its cognitive and social aspects. These are closely associated with teachers' beliefs and emotions; what they think and feel about their practices. The more central a belief and more connected to their emotions, the more influential it is to their identities (Barcelos, 2015).

Because teacher identities are social, as we saw with learner identities earlier, they are always negotiated with others in sociocultural and geopolitical spaces and are thus ideological. Those involved in language education (including learners) have varying views about what is right and wrong and what should and what should not happen in classrooms, schools, and the profession as a whole, and some people have more power than others to make decisions regarding the outcome of these dilemmas, which shift over historical time and social context.

The negotiation of identities in these times and contexts can lead to both struggle and harmony. At times they are contested and resisted, by self and others. When teachers ask themselves questions about who they are and what they do, sometimes the answers clash with their beliefs and personal ideological assumptions. For example, they may be teaching a nationally prescribed syllabus or following institutional assessment procedures that do not align with their own ideas about best and fair practice. Students, or their parents, or institutional administrators may also have views about a teacher (e.g., how 'good' they are) that are contrary to those of the teacher. In these cases, when tensions arise from within or from outside, teachers may be able to overcome the identity conflicts through their own actions (possibly with organizational support), but this is not always feasible.

At other times, teachers' identities are accepted, acknowledged, and valued, by self and others. In these circumstances, teachers are recognized as making a contribution, their beliefs and practices match those of colleagues in their schools, and they align what they do and believe and feel with the policies of macro institutions such as Ministries

From Research to Implications

of Education and even governments. They also find themselves aligning with ideological structures to do with, for example, teacher professional development, language and diversity, and particular sociocultural values.

Considering the conceptualization so far, it follows that teacher identities are dynamic and multiple. Different teacher identities are negotiated and foregrounded at different times and in different contexts depending on who they are with and what they are doing — for example, facilitating classroom activities (instructor), designing a curriculum innovation (curriculum developer), assessing learners' written work (assessor), conducting an action research project (researcher), providing pastoral care for students (counsellor), or managing a department (leader).

There is obviously considerable overlap among these identities, so teacher identities are also potentially often hybrid. A teacher presenting a workshop on the findings of an action research project, for example, is both teacher and researcher. But identities change. Short term, discursively in social interaction, a teacher might shift from displaying a teacher rather than a researcher identity, even during a workshop.

Over time, a teacher might relinquish much classroom teaching and take on more administrative or management duties, thus becoming an educational leader. The teacher–leader hybrid identity would now shift the leader component to a core identity position.

As we have emphasized before, that identities are constructed discursively in social interaction reflects a poststructuralist perspective on identity. Language, as one available semiotic resource, is central in understanding the relationship between teachers and their social worlds. It is through the language choices they make that they negotiate a sense of self.

But teachers also take part in interactions and relationships with non-human objects and materials and with ecological spaces in which they are 'entangled', both micro and macro. An obvious example of material interaction is the use of classroom teaching materials. But materiality extends to the arrangement of things (e.g., furniture in classrooms, mobile phones) and spaces (e.g., meeting rooms, group-work

20

From Research to Implications

configurations) and their interaction with teachers' lives and practices in the process of identities construction.

Further Reading

Barkhuizen, G. (Ed.). (2017). *Reflections on language teacher identity research*. New York, NY: Routledge.

Sample Study

Dikilitaş, K., & Yaylı, D. (2018). Teachers' professional identity development through action research. *English Language Teaching Journal, 72*(4), 415–424.

F. Implications of Identity Research for Application

We started Part 1 by addressing some big issues in research on identity in language teaching and learning based on the work of De Costa and Norton (2016). The aim of this section was to provide an overview of some of the recent issues and developments in language learning and teaching identity research and to emphasize the point that what happens in classrooms is influenced by what happens in the world outside of classrooms and institutions, particularly with regard to the constantly changing multiple identities of teachers and learners.

We then turned to Norton's (2013) conceptualization of language *learner* identity, a poststructuralist perspective on identity that emphasizes people's understanding of their relationship to the world, thus clearly aligning with the recent research trends. Her conceptualization provides us with a definition of learner identity that informs both the design of the activities in the next part of the book as well as the discussion of curriculum and research in the parts that follow. Since *teacher* identity is so central to understanding language learning and teaching, we then looked at Barkhuizen's (2017) conceptualization of language teacher identity, making connections with learner identity along the way.

From Research to Implications

As teachers and teacher-researchers, our interest lies in how language and identity relate to what we do in classrooms and schools—in other words, the implications of the research and its associated conceptualizations presented earlier. In the past (and still today in many geopolitical regions around the world), identity has not been perceived to be something that teachers needed to pay much attention to. There has been no systematic examination of its relationship to the language being taught, and learners have not been given opportunities to reflect on their changing identities and what this might mean for them as language learners. Teachers have gone about their business without considering their own changing identities, and big issues such as globalization, intersectionality, links to other disciplines, and even relations of power in the lives of learners have not been considered in the micro, meso, and macro contexts in which their learning has taken place.

Increasingly more often, however, teachers and researchers (and teacher education programs) have come to recognize that learning and teaching practices are intertwined with social relationships, institutional practices, and ideologies that extend well beyond classrooms and schools—and that learners' and teachers' identities are implicated. This, we hope, has been the clear message in Part 1. We articulate the implications of this message in the form of four facets of identity (based on Benson, Barkhuizen, Bodycott, & Brown, 2013; Harré, 2001). These facets emphasize different, though very much interrelated, dimensions of an individual's identity, particularly their interaction with other people, institutions, and social structures—real and imagined. We express the facets here in terms of *communicating identity*, a social action.

1. *Reflexing identities*

   - refers to 'who we think we are'
   - is the learners' view of the self
   - includes language learners' conceptions of their abilities, capacities, and competencies

From Research to Implications

- includes linguistic self-concept — conceptions of language knowledge and skills and ability to use it in various contexts of interaction
- represents the inner self, which is multiple and variable

2. *Projecting identities*

- refers to 'how we want others to see us'
- is the public representation of the outer self
- refers to learners' (un)consciously projected identity to others
- recognizes a potential gap between projected and reflexive identities
- acknowledges that language is important for projecting identities
- values other semiotic resources (e.g., appearance, gesture, dress)
- represents the outer self, which is multiple and variable

3. *Recognizing identities*

- refers to 'how others see us'
- is the counterpart of projected identities
- includes the way learners' projected identities are understood and acted upon by others in specific social contexts
- could be identities others "ascribe or attribute" to us (Blommaert, 2006, p. 238)
- are potentially 'imposed' identities, which may not be compatible with reflexive or projected identities
- has implications (both ascribed and imposed) for reflexive identities

4. *Imagining identities*

- refers to 'how we imagine ourselves' in other times and/or spaces
- includes learners' imagined self, participating in imagined (target language) communities
- includes possible future selves

23

From Research to Implications

- "the ideal selves that we would very much like to become and the selves we are afraid of becoming" (Markus & Nurius, 1986, p. 954)

To further emphasize the identity facets' interrelatedness, spread across all four are the familiar identity categories and resources available to us in our sociocultural contexts that we use to talk about identity, such as cultural identity, and gender, social class, and religious identity. All the activities in Part 2 focus on one or more of these identity categories. Sometimes one category is the focus, but in other activities more than one identity category is covered. Block (2007) distinguishes among a number of different types of language learner identities, and although he presents these separately, he cautions that it is difficult to consider one without taking into account the others (see *intersectionality* earlier). The following brief descriptions, probably because they are brief, are potentially contentious, and have been defined variously from different theoretical perspectives. But they will suffice for the purposes of the activities that follow (p. 43):

1. *Ethnic identity*: shared history, descent, belief systems, practices, language, and religion, all associated with a cultural group
2. *Racial identity*: biological or genetic make-up
3. *National identity*: shared history, descent, belief systems, practices, language associated with a nation state
4. *Migrant identity*: ways of living in a new country, on a scale ranging from classic immigrant to transmigrant (those "straddling geographical, social and psychological borders," p. 33)
5. *Gender identity*: nature of conformity to socially constructed notions of femininities and masculinities, as well as orientations to sexuality and sexual activity
6. *Social class identity*: income level, occupation, education and symbolic behavior (e.g., language, clothing, pastimes)
7. *Language identity*: relationship between one's sense of self and different means of communication, understood in terms of language, a dialect or sociolect, as well as multimodality

Other categories that have appeared in research and discussions of learner and teacher identity are *age* and *religious* identity, and these are also included as the focus of some of the activities in Part 2. Like the other categories, descriptions and understandings of what these categories actually mean are changing as new theoretical perspectives and research findings emerge over time.

G. Looking Ahead: Communicating Identities

In Part 2 we move from the implications of the research and its associated conceptualizations to application in classroom practice. We link the main implications of the research, in the form of the four facets of identity, to the activities in four sections.

Part 2

From Implications to Application

A. Introduction

Part 1 ended with the implications of language learner and teacher identity research in the form of four facets of identity. In other words, the facets represent the implications. These facets emphasize the main research and conceptual themes concerning language learner and teacher identity outlined in Part 1, that is, that identities are negotiated and constructed discursively in particular time and social scales of context. In other words, we communicate our identities, to others and ourselves, as we interact with other people and material objects in the world. The activities in this Part 2 draw on the research reviewed in Part 1 and its implications (i.e., the four identity facets). Thus, the activities are linked to the research via their association with the identity facets.

Organization of the Activities in Part 2

Table 2.1 shows the link between the implications (i.e., the facets of identity) and the activities. For each facet we highlight the key concepts associated with it and then provide a set of activities that enables readers to explore these aspects of identity further. For each facet there are 12 activities.

The four sets of activities are sequenced according to the order of the identity facets: reflexing, projecting, recognizing, and imagining. Although the facets are very much interrelated, this sequence is logical. *Reflexing* identity begins with the individual's inner self—how the learner or teacher views their own identity. Next, *projecting* identity moves outward as the individual engages with others in social interaction and thereby projects or represents their identity publicly. This projected identity is received or *recognized* by others, who then attribute characteristics to the individual

From Implications to Application

Table 2.1 Link between research implications and activities

Implications (facets of identity)	Key concepts	Activities
Reflexing identities	• 'Who we think we are' • Self-concept • Inner self • Multiple and variable	Activities 1–12
Projecting identities	• 'How we want others to see us' • Projected identity to others • Public representation • Outer self • Language is important	Activities 13–24
Recognizing identities	• 'How others see us' • Counterpart of projected identities • Ascribed or attributed identities • Imposed identities	Activities 25–36
Imagining identities	• 'How we imagine ourselves' • Participating in imagined communities • Possible future selves • Ideal selves • Feared selves	Activities 37–48

(i.e., what kind of person they are). Sometimes recognizing identities are imposed even without consideration or acknowledgement of an individual's reflexive self. Finally, *imagining* identities involves an individual imagining themselves in other places and (future) times, in imagined communities not immediately present.

Although we have ordered the identity facets and the associated activities in this way, it is important to emphasize their interrelatedness. Just to illustrate, how others view an individual (i.e., recognized identity) will have an effect on that individual's perception of self as well. And how a person projects a particular identity might not always be recognized

27

From Implications to Application

the way that person intends. The 12 activities assigned to a particular facet (e.g., *reflexing*), therefore, may well include aspects (key concepts) of the other three identity facets, but any particular identity facet (e.g., *reflexing*) will most saliently be evident in its 12 assigned activities.

A final note about the nature and structure of the activities. They are resources that you can draw on to structure and guide your learners' exploration of their and other people's identities. The activities have been designed to promote as far as possible genuine communication. Many are communicative tasks in the sense that they involve an information gap and learners' exchange of information. A number are creative tasks (e.g., tasks in which learners design or select an image to visually capture aspects of their identities). Some tasks involve learners in making observations of identity in language use, and in this way they aim to foster their abilities to explore identity and language at the same time.

The activities are structured in the same way, as follows:

1. An *introduction* provides some background information about the identity-related content of the activity and briefly indicates what the activity involves.
2. Next comes information about the specific *aims* of the activity, as well as suggestions regarding the appropriate *level* (elementary, intermediate, or advanced) and *time* allocation. The required *materials* and lesson *preparation* are also listed here.
3. A box describes the activity's focus on *language practice*. It consists of three parts, as illustrated here:

Language practice	
Skills?	listening, speaking, multimodal activity
What?	listening to a lecture, analyzing various identity factors and weighing their significance, creating a multimodal collage, explaining its significance to the class
How?	whole-class instruction, working on the collage independently, describing in groups and to the whole class

From Implications to Application

- What *skills* are the focus of the activity? Most of the activities include practice of multiple skills, but here we list those that are most significant in the activity.
- *What* about these skills do students focus on? Here we are a little more specific about the classroom work that involves the skills.
- *How* are the activities carried out? Some indication is given here about the students' work arrangements—working by themselves independently, in pairs or groups, or as a whole class.

4. The *procedures* and suggestions for facilitating the class activity are then described in order.
5. In some activities possible *extensions* or *variations* are recommended.
6. The *teacher reflection* then follows. This gives you the opportunity to reflect in your own time on your professional identity. The reflection is closely related to the substance of the activity.
7. The final section includes the materials, such as worksheets, that are required for the activity.

Last, it is important to be flexible by being willing to adapt the activity, especially in terms of:

- *Your learning and teaching context*: The nature of the students, the facilities and teaching equipment available, the length of the lessons (and the school day), the technology available, and the support offered for training and professional development vary in different contexts, such as community schools, secondary schools, private language schools, and higher education institutions, for example.
- *The English proficiency level of your learners*: For each activity we have stipulated only three general levels of English proficiency: elementary, intermediate, or advanced. You will be familiar with your learners and with your learning and teaching context and thus best positioned to adapt the activities to fit the level of your learners,

29

From Implications to Application

for example, by adding or deleting content or by adjusting for time available and class size.

- *The timing of the activities*: We have suggested time periods for the entire lesson and for some of the activities therein. Again, these are suggestions, and you will know best how to adjust these according to your local circumstances.
- *The size of the class*: As with time and proficiency levels, the size of the class will have an effect on how activities potentially unfold. Some activities may not be appropriate at all for your context because class sizes are too large, but others may be possible if the class is broken up into small groups. If your classes are too small for any full activity, then only some aspects of the activity could be selected.

B. Reflexing Identities

Table 2.2 Reflexing identities: Activity titles and aims

Activity	Title	Aims
Activity 1	This Is (Not) Like Me	• To familiarize students with the course book • To get students thinking about their own identities • To practice using adjectives associated with identity categories (age, ethnicity)
Activity 2	Celebrating Birthdays	• To revise the use of past and future tenses • To describe birthday celebrations using appropriate vocabulary • To compare responses to a sentence completion task

Activity	Title	Aims
Activity 3	What Makes Me Me?	• To consider the various factors that influence the make up of our identity • To select those that individual students believe have had a more prominent role than others and justifying this selection • To use photos, magazine pictures, drawings, colors, or words to construct a collage that illustrates student identity • To explain the collage to the class
Activity 4	Tweeting	• To identify the gist of a news story • To summarize the story in 140 characters or less • To critique another student's summary
Activity 5	Memories and Smells	• To use the correct tense to reflect past and present actions and feelings • To compare and contrast perceptions of smell • To tell stories from the past
Activity 6	Maps of the World	• To reflect critically on different perspectives of the world map • To write basic notes and share information in groups and with the whole class • To consider how representations of the world may impact on national identity, world-views, and perspectives
Activity 7	Using Our Brains!	• To think critically and broadly about a concept • To consider the merit of thoughts and ideas • To reflect on how flexible students are to think differently

(Continued)

Table 2.2 (Continued)

Activity	Title	Aims
Activity 8	The Genders of Objects	• To review grammatical gender • To consider perceptions of gender in objects • To critically examine imposed gendered identities
Activity 9	Food and Identity	• To point out differences between formal and informal language • To practice summarizing • To show students they can work out what a word means from the context • to reflect on the students' cultural practices regarding food
Activity 10	Author Presence	• To consider how writers construct identities in academic writing • To reflect on personal preferences for referring to self as author
Activity 11	Chickens in Cages	• To identify arguments for and against a farming practice • To identify differences between formal and informal writing (vocabulary and grammar)
Activity 12	My Ideal Holiday	• To think about the kind of travel students enjoy • To analyze why this travel appeals to them • To conceptualize their ideal holiday • To cooperate within a group to develop a description of an ideal trip

From Implications to Application

Activity 1: This Is (Not) Like Me

Introduction

Students usually have access to a course book or textbook in their language course, whether it is hard copy or electronic. This short activity asks students to flip through their course book for a few minutes to examine images or any other diagrams, keywords, figures, and so on that may or may not reflect how they see themselves — their identities. Students write down why this is the case and share their responses in pairs. The activity could serve as a warm-up activity at the start of a unit of work.

Aim:	- To familiarize students with the course book
	- To get students thinking about their own identities
	- To practice using adjectives associated with identity categories (age, ethnicity)
Level:	Elementary
Time:	40 minutes
Materials:	Course book or textbook or online learning platform that all students have access to. Magazines or newspapers can be used if neither the course book nor online material is available.
Preparation:	- Ensure that materials are available.
	- Prepare sample responses of your own to illustrate activity to students.

Language practice	
Skills?	reading, sentence level writing
What?	skimming text, expressing a reason, using adjectives
How?	skim reading independently, pair work

33

From Implications to Application

Procedure

1. Ask students to take out their course books or textbooks (or have them log in to a common online learning platform or distribute a magazine or newspaper).
2. Give students about 10 minutes to page through the course book.
3. Students will pick out five images, which could be of people or animals or objects, and might consist of:

   - photographs
   - drawings
   - diagrams
   - figures
   - keywords
   - shapes
   - colors

4. For each of the five images, students write down the page number and then complete the sentence, writing it next to the page number: *This is like me because* . . .
5. Provide the students with an example or two of your own. Some possible examples:

   - A picture of a woman: *This is like me because I am female.*
   - A photograph of a cow in a field: *This is like me because the grass is green, and I like nature and want to save the planet.*
   - An advertisement for a new car: *This is like me because I plan to be a mechanic one day.*

6. They then find five more images, write the page number for each, and complete and write down the sentence: *This is not like me because* . . .
7. After students have their 10 sentences, put them into pairs. Each student has a turn to show one of their 10 images (referring to page number) to their partner, and the partner then has to guess if the image *is* or *is not* like their partner and then *why* or *why not.*

34

From Implications to Application

8. When students have had a few turns each, stop the pair work.
9. This might be a good time to explain to the class the meaning of the word *identity*. You could simply say, "Identity is who we are, how we see others, and how others see us."
10. And let the students know that identity will be a part of many of the activities in your future classes.

Teacher Reflection

Next time you flip through the materials and documents you come across in your professional life, think about how the images, keywords, and diagrams reflect how you see yourself as a teacher, administrator, or researcher. Such materials may include:

- your course books
- syllabus documents
- policy statements
- institutional websites
- institutional Facebook pages
- school newsletters, notices, and memos
- students' work

Activity 2: Celebrating Birthdays

Introduction

Birthdays are usually a significant day for people. It is a time when people show that we are special and important in their lives. Different cultures have different ways of celebrating birthdays, and often families have their own special birthday traditions as well. Memories of birthday celebrations are often a treasured part of our identities. In this activity, students are asked to talk about past birthday celebrations and how they would like to mark their birthdays in the future. Students complete a number of simple sentences in writing and compare responses in pairs.

35

From Implications to Application

Aim:	- To revise the use of past and future tenses
	- To describe birthday celebrations using appropriate vocabulary
	- To compare responses to a sentence completion task
Level:	Elementary
Time:	40 minutes
Materials:	A worksheet with questions and sentences to complete is provided.
Preparation:	Prepare copies of the worksheet for each student.

Language practice	
Skills?	speaking, vocabulary, writing
What?	using past and future tenses to describe past and future birthday celebrations, completing sentences on a worksheet, comparing responses
How?	completing the worksheet independently, comparting worksheet responses in pairs, reading responses to the whole class

Procedure

1. Introduce the activity by discussing with students how birthdays are celebrated differently around the world. In Vietnam, for instance, everyone's birthday is on New Year's Day, and children are given money in red envelopes by older people. In Hungary, there is a custom that someone will tug on your ears while they sing a song that translates as "God bless you. May you live so long that your ears reach your ankles!" In other parts of the world, people start their birthdays by visiting places of worship.
2. Ask students to talk about traditional ways of celebrating birthdays in their own culture. Do their families have special traditions?
3. Hand out the worksheet, one to each student.

36

From Implications to Application

4. Ask students to complete the worksheet.
5. In pairs, ask students to read their completed worksheet sentence by sentence, stopping after each sentence to compare responses. How are the birthday celebrations similar and different?
6. Call on students to volunteer to read responses of their choice to the whole class.

Extension

More advanced students might want to investigate the significance of certain ages in different cultures. For example, the 13th birthday of Jewish children has great significance, while the Dutch pay special attention to the Crown Years (e.g., 5, 10, 15, 20). There is, of course, the legal significance of turning 18 or 21. Students might also be interested in looking at different zodiac systems such as the Chinese and Western systems, where your sign depends on your birth date. Students could examine the beliefs behind the systems. On a more personal level, students could write about a particularly significant birthday they have celebrated.

Teacher Reflection

Is there a tradition in your institution (or other institutions you have worked in) of celebrating teachers' birthdays? In some cultures and institutions, colleagues bring cake to school to celebrate a teacher's birthday with morning coffee or afternoon tea. Sometimes it is the teacher who brings the cake.

1. What do you think the purpose of such institution-based celebrations might be?
2. What benefits are there for the teacher celebrating the birthday?
3. What benefits are there for the other colleagues?
4. Why would some teachers (or you) prefer *not* to celebrate their birthdays in the workplace?
5. Do you tell your students when it is your birthday? Why or why not?

From Implications to Application

Materials

Worksheet

What was the first birthday you can remember? What do you remember about it?

1. I remember the birthday when I _____.

2. Why was it special? _____.

What was the worst birthday you can remember?

3. My worst birthday was when I _____.

4. Why was it a bad day? _____.

What was the best birthday gift you got?

5. The best birthday gift I got was _____.

6. Why was it special? _____.

What are you going to do on your next birthday?

7. On my next birthday, I am _____.

What presents will you ask for?

8. I will ask for _____.

How will you celebrate your 75th birthday?

9. I will _____.

Activity 3: What Makes Me Me?

Introduction

In this activity, learners reflect on their own identities. Different factors that contribute to our concept of self are considered. Students consider these factors and raise other influences that they believe have affected their self-concept. They design a collage that they feel best illustrates who they are. They are then given an opportunity to describe their collage to the class.

From Implications to Application

Aim:	- To consider the various factors that influence the make up our identity
	- To select those that individual students believe have had a more prominent role than others and justifying this selection
	- To use photos, magazine pictures, drawings, colors, or words to construct a collage that illustrates student identity
	- To explain the collage to the class
Level:	Intermediate
Time:	60 minutes
Materials:	Magazines, newspapers, and photos that students can cut up; colored pens and pencils; a large piece of paper or cardboard for each student; glue; and scissors.
Preparation:	- Tell students before the lesson that in this activity, they will be talking about what is important to them.
	- Ask them in the previous lesson to bring photos or other materials they will use to make a collage.

Language practice	
Skills?	listening, speaking, multimodal activity
What?	listening to a lecture, analyzing various identity factors and weighing their significance, creating a multimodal collage, explaining its significance to class
How?	whole-class instruction, working on the collage independently, describing in groups and to whole class

Procedure

1. Talk to the students about our sense of identity. You can illustrate this with examples. Being a teacher might give someone a

39

From Implications to Application

sense of purpose and fulfilment, and this becomes central to this person's identity. Perhaps someone is very proud of his or her country, culture, or language, and this shapes the kind of person they are. However, others might be impatient of traditional ways and believe that allegiance to one country is not as important as empathy with all people. If you are comfortable doing so, you might share some of the factors that make up who you are with your students.

2. The following facets have been identified in the book:

   a. culture
   b. language
   c. gender
   d. age
   e. social class
   f. religion
   g. sexuality
   h. nationality
   i. ethnicity
   j. race

There are, of course, many more such as personality, interests, abilities, environment, and family, to name just a few. You could suggest a few from the list above and then ask the students to brainstorm other options.

3. Write all the answers on the board.
4. Then tell the students that they are going to make a collage using photos, words, pictures, and colors.

   a. A collage is an artwork made from an assemblage of different forms. This enables students to create a new whole.
   b. There are various examples of collages that people have made representing themselves, and there are excellent examples of these on the internet (search 'identity collage').
   c. A student might, for example, draw a picture representing him or herself. There might be photos of family, pictures of people

From Implications to Application

in jobs the student is aiming to qualify for, lines of poetry, sports teams, landscapes, drawings, and colors. The writing need not be in English.

5. While students are working on their collage, encourage them to ask and answer questions about each other's developing collage. If the class is small enough ask each student to show their collage to the class and explain its significance, asking: "How does this collage represent who you are?"
6. In bigger classes students can present to each other in small groups while you move around the room listening to various explanations.
7. Ask the students to file the collages carefully or put them up on the classroom wall, if possible, as you might want to revisit them for another lesson later (see Extension).

Extension

This activity lends itself very easily to extension work. Although it is aimed at intermediate students, it can easily be tailored for the elementary level using fewer categories and making the discussion less complex. Conversely, more advanced students might explore the categories at a deeper level and introduce philosophical or political considerations. The activity might also be done using technological tools (e.g., PowerPoint, iMovie, PowToon) rather than conventional pen, pictures, and paper.

Teacher Reflection

This lesson helps students to develop an understanding of the complex nature of identity. It might offer you an opportunity to explore your own identity. What makes you tick? What collage of your life and identity would you construct? What would it look like? Who would you want to show it to? Who would you definitely not show it to?

From Implications to Application

Activity 4: Tweeting

Introduction

Some of your students are likely to be one of the 100 million daily active users of Twitter. Twitter is a social networking site that can be used to get the latest news, follow the lives of high-profile celebrities, or just stay in touch with friends. It is also used by politicians around the world to express their views. Using social media is very much part of our students' daily lives, and how they express themselves on these sites is a reflection of their identity. It enables them to express who they are and what their views of the world are. It also illustrates the fact that ordinary people (not necessarily journalists or celebrities) can share breaking news. In this activity, students use the Twitter convention of 140 characters to summarize a news item.

Aim:	- To identify the gist of a news story
	- To summarize the story in 140 characters or less
	- To critique another student's summary
Level:	Intermediate
Time:	60 minutes
Materials:	A worksheet is provided. It uses tweets of important news events. However, you might want to replace the items in Section A with more recent items or ones that are more relevant for your student cohort.
Preparation:	Prepare copies of the worksheet below for each student and update tweets if necessary.

Language practice	
Skills?	reading, writing, speaking
What?	discussing well known tweets, writing own tweet (summarizing), critiquing other students' summaries
How?	whole-class discussions, completing worksheet in pairs

From Implications to Application

Procedure

1. Discuss Twitter with the class. You might ask them if any of them use Twitter. If there are members of the class who do, ask them to talk about their use. You will probably find that even if students don't use it themselves, they are familiar with its use. Twitter creates content that is very easy and quick to read because messages may have no more than 140 characters. Messages spread very quickly when users retweet messages to their own followers. Some tweets have been retweeted over four and a half millions times. If you have internet access in your classroom and a data projector, you could briefly demonstrate Twitter use to the whole class.

2. Distribute the worksheets and ask students to work in pairs to complete Section A. They could work independently, but discussion in pairs may be helpful for remembering the content of the tweet.

3. Then initiate a class discussion about the tweets they have just read.

   a. Can they remember the incidents?
   b. Are there other famous tweets that have made an impression on them?
   c. Which of the tweets tell us something about the identity of the tweeter?

   Ask them to share these recollections with the class. If there is time, they might want to search online using their phones to find the relevant tweet.

4. Then ask each student to find a news article online that is of interest to them. It could be in any area, such as politics, sport, or entertainment.

5. Ask the students to complete Section B of the worksheet, first by themselves and then with a partner.

6. Ask students to exchange worksheets and URLs and then to read the relevant article and comment on how well the tweet summarized the article.

From Implications to Application

7. To end the class, ask students to comment on the following:

    a. When sending a tweet, what are some of the personal risks involved?

    b. What might a tweet reveal about the sender that they could later regret?

Teacher Reflection

Write three 140-character tweets that describe your reflections on this activity.

1. _____

2. _____

3. _____

Materials

Worksheet

Section A

Can you remember the incident referred to in these tweets. Count the number of characters used. Would you have lengthened or shortened the tweet?

Tweet	Number of characters
There's a plane in the Hudson. I'm on the ferry going to pick up the people. Crazy.	
Boris Johnson and Jeremy Hunt through to the final round of Conservative Party leadership contest to become next PM.	

From Implications to Application

Tweet	Number of characters
NHS opens first gambling clinic for children. Some 55,000 children classed as having an addiction with online gambling sites blamed.	
LIMONADA	
The Prince of Wales is delighted to announce the engagement of Prince William to Miss Catherine Middleton.	
New emperor. New era. And new challenges for the country.	
"It is in the best interests of the country for a new prime minister to lead." UK PM May announces she will resign 7 June.	
Ruling party in Turkey set to lose city of Istanbul after re-run mayoral election in big blow for President Erdogan.	
You are witnessing the single greatest WITCH HUNT in American political history—led by some very bad and conflicted people.	

Section B

Find a news event online that is of interest to you. Copy the URL into the box and then summarize the article in a tweet. Count the number of characters. When you have done this, exchange the worksheet with another student. Find the article your partner read and look at the tweet. Do you think the article has been well summarized? What would you have done differently? Discuss your answers with your partner.

45

From Implications to Application

URL of article	Tweet (yours)	Number of characters

Sources

https://en.wikipedia.org/wiki/List_of_most-retweeted_tweets

https://twitter.com/BBCBreaking/status/1142831589543546882?ref_src=twsrc%5Egoogle%7Ctwcamp%5Eserp%7Ctwgr%5Etweet

www.lifewire.com/what-exactly-is-twitter-2483331

Activity 5: Memories and Smells

Introduction

Our memories help make us who we are and affect the way we behave. If our memories of a place or time are pleasant, we tend to view that time and place favorably and return to these memories regularly. However, if our memories are unpleasant, we often have negative associations with places and people and do not wish to revisit the memories. In this activity, students sample various smells, list their preferences, and compare their perceptions with those of other students.

Aim:	- To use the correct tense to reflect past and present actions and feelings
	- To compare and contrast perceptions of smell
	- To tell stories from the past
Level:	Intermediate
Time:	60 minutes

46

From Implications to Application

Materials: Items that have a strong smell such as a can of deodorant, spices, or flowers

Preparation: Think of smells that bring back memories to you that you can share with your class.

Language practice	
Skills?	listening, speaking, writing
What?	listening to factual information, comparing information, telling stories, writing brief explanations
How?	whole-class listening, working in pairs, independent writing, whole-class question and answer

Procedure

1. Tell the class that according to scientists, our sense of smell is more closely linked with memory than any of our other senses. We often have a strong emotional reaction to smells. Probably this is because of the associations that we have with those smells. Apparently, different smells often take us back to our childhood. This is because the brain stores scents in the same part as it does long-term memories.
2. Ask the class to give examples of smells from their childhood that bring back strong memories. Are the memories good or bad?
3. Then pass around the items you have brought to class and ask students which of the different smells they like. Although there are some smells that most people like, such as the smell of baking bread and freshly mown lawns, there are many other smells where people are divided as to whether they find them unpleasant or not.
4. Give the class a chance to discuss the items you have brought (this could be done in groups in a large class). Which smells seem to be popular? Do students have memories of any of these smells?
5. It will become clear that not everyone likes the same smells. Ask students to come up with examples of smells that some people

47

From Implications to Application

really like and other people really dislike. Some of these might include:

- incense, frying onions, a match that has just been blown out, chlorine, curry, new car smell, cigarette smoke, mothballs, lavender, gasoline, cinnamon.

6. Write the list on the board—it does not have to be very long. Seven or eight examples should be enough.
7. From the list ask each student to choose a smell that they like and a smell that they don't like and write them down.
8. Next to their choices the students need to explain why they think they like or don't like a particular smell. For example, they might like the smell of cigarettes because they remind the student of times spent with an adult they liked who smoked. Someone might dislike the smell of cinnamon because it reminds him or her of a dish they had to eat as a child that they didn't like.
9. Then ask each student to find another student who also likes or dislikes the same smells that they do. They then compare reasons for liking or disliking them.
10. Ask the class which are the most popular or unpopular smells and to share their stories as to why they like or dislike a particular smell.

Extension/Variation

1. At elementary level, you could put a number of items with a strong smell in brown paper bags. Students smell the bags to identify the objects (e.g., different kinds of flowers, fruit, spices, herbs). The names of the items can then be written on the board and students can vote to find out which of the smells are the most and least popular.
2. Students at a more advanced level could be asked to search for examples of the description of smells in stories and poetry (they could use Google) and how these arouse memories (e.g., how the smell of

From Implications to Application

blood can bring back the horror of war or an accident). They could then write a poem or short story in which smell plays a central role.

Teacher Reflection

1. Have you always wanted to be a language teacher?
2. Do you have any memories from your childhood that prompted you to become a language teacher?
3. During the activity, did *you* experience any smells that triggered a significant memory for you? How did this memory make you feel? Did the memory have anything to do with language, learning, or teaching?

Activity 6: Maps of the World

Introduction

This activity encourages students to look at the world in different ways, prompted by varying organization of world maps. They consider the size and importance of countries, including their own, and their place within it. The activity involves note taking, the sharing of information, and face-to-face question and answer interaction.

Aim:	- To reflect critically on different perspectives of the world map
	- To write basic notes and share information in groups and with the whole class
	- To consider how representations of the world may impact on national identity, world-views, and perspectives
Level:	Intermediate
Time:	50 minutes
Materials:	A traditional map of the world showing Greenland at the top. An alternative map of the world, for

49

From Implications to Application

example, a map of the world showing Australia at the top. Possible sources:

- www.nationalgeographic.org/education/class room-resources/mapping/
- www.flourish.org/upsidedownmap/

Preparation: Find the two maps, either physical maps or maps on a website(s).

Language practice	
Skills?	writing, speaking, visual literacy
What?	note taking, sentence writing, reporting back orally
How?	write answers to questions on worksheet, report back to whole class, whole-class instruction, group work, mix and mingle to ask and answer questions

Procedure

1. Tell students that the topic is 'countries of origin and maps'. Show them the traditional map of the world.
2. Give out the Maps Worksheet. Students write sentence endings for Part 1.
3. Invite students to read out their responses to Part 1. Highlight ways of describing geographical location and write these on the board.
4. Introduce the expression 'where a country is in the world' and explain its two possible meanings: geographical location and views on importance.
5. Show the students the alternative map of the world that shows Australia at the top. Introduce the idea that this map may change people's perspectives. For example, a country looks closer or more important.
6. Put students in groups of two or three to exchange ideas using Part 2 on the Worksheet.
7. Ask one student from each group to report on the ideas discussed. Highlight ways of describing geographical location, distance, and importance. Write brief notes on the board.

50

From Implications to Application

8. Get students to work independently and revise and expand their individual notes on their countries of origin using Part 3 of the worksheet.
9. Then get students to mix and mingle using Part 4 of the worksheet. Students ask and answer questions either to learn about countries other than their own or to compare ideas about the country of origin they have in common.

Extension/Variation

1. For this activity you could use historical maps of the world, such as a map of Mexico in 1824 showing California as part of Mexico. Students can search websites for historical maps relevant to their interests for use in class discussions. For an advanced class, you might include a reading, such as *How the North Ended Up on Top of the Map*: http://america.aljazeera.com/opinions/2014/2/maps-cartogra phycolonialismnortheurocentricglobe.html.
2. Terms, such as *Far East, Middle East, Eastern or Western Europe,* and *first world or third world* can be introduced and discussed. Does everyone agree on how these terms are used?
3. Ask students to discuss a shared country of origin with family members and friends and report back to class the next day. Do younger and older people have similar views on 'where the country is' in the world?

Teacher Reflection

Consider these three questions:

1. Has this activity raised your awareness of how your students' countries of origin may be perceived in your school and community? Do you agree with any prevalent perceptions?
2. Consider ways that your students' national identities may interact (interfere?) with their language learning.
3. Do you think you project your national identity in your teaching in any way?

From Implications to Application

Materials

Worksheet

Part 1

Write endings for these sentence starters:

>*My country of origin is* _____.
>*This country is* _____ *(geographical location).*

Part 2

Discuss and note down your group's ideas on the following questions:

- Does the alternative map change your perspectives of where countries are in the world?
- How important are some of the countries you see?
- How large or small are some countries?
- How far or close from your country are other countries?

Prepare to report your group's ideas to the class.

Part 3

Review your notes from Part 1. This time, revise and expand your notes on your country of origin to include:

- more detail on geographical location.
- views on where the country 'is in the world' — and why.

Part 4

Do you come from different countries of origin? Find out about the countries of origin of other students in the class. Ask these questions:

- What's your country of origin?
- Where is it in the world?

From Implications to Application

Do you share the same country of origin? Find out how other students describe the country. Do you have similar descriptions and views? Ask these questions:

- What did you write?
- Where do you think (the country) is in the world?

Activity 7: Using Our Brains!

Introduction

Some students are confident about their ability to think logically and clearly. Others are not so sure and would rather wait to hear what their fellow students say before they express an opinion. The way we think is a large part of who and what we are. Our confidence in our ideas and their validity gives us agency. Edward De Bono (1982) is regarded as one of the world's leading authorities in the field of creative and conceptual thinking. He believes that people who are confident about their thinking often come up with one idea and don't really explore any options. Students need to be encouraged to think more widely and to consider different ideas. Other people have good ideas too! As De Bono noted, *If you never change your mind, why have one?* In this activity, students are asked to work in groups to consider an idea from different perspectives, and then to consider other perspectives of the same idea.

[Source: De Bono, E. (1982). *De Bono's thinking course*. Chatham: BBC Books.]

Aim:	- To think critically and broadly about a concept
	- To consider the merit of thoughts and ideas
	- To reflect on how flexible students are to think differently
Level:	Intermediate
Time:	60 minutes
Materials:	A number of different propositions and concepts that students can consider. Examples have been

53

From Implications to Application

provided. A worksheet is provided for the input of the combined groups.

Preparation: - Prepare an example of what you would like students to do (see example later) and make copies for each group.
- Prepare copies of a worksheet for the input of the combined groups.

Language practice	
Skills	listening, speaking, critical thinking
What?	listing pros, cons, and ideas in writing; considering the pros, cons, and ideas of others; evaluating pros, cons, and ideas; justifying positions
How?	whole-class discussion, group discussion, combined group discussion

Procedure

1. Talk to students about the way they think. You might, for example, ask them about what they do when they are asked to give their opinions on a topic. Do they come up with an answer and then work on justifying this, or do they think of a number of options?
2. Introduce students to the idea of PMI (plus, minus, and interesting): plus stands for the good points of an idea, minus stands for the bad points, and interesting stands for interesting points.
3. Hand out examples of what you want students to do. See responses in the Materials below to *Only one kind of car should be manufactured worldwide*.
4. Then choose a proposition to put to the students. You can use one of the examples provided (see Materials) or one of your own. Before you start work, ask students to indicate whether they are in favor of the proposal or not.
5. Divide students into groups (three or four students). Then randomly assign one of the three approaches (plus, minus, interesting) to each group. Ask them to come up with a number of points in relation

54

From Implications to Application

to the proposition. Remind them that the points must support the PMI they have been given, not their personal preferences. This is an exercise about thinking differently. Remind the interesting group that they are not there to support or oppose the idea.

6. Give the groups enough time to come up with a number of points. It would be a good idea for the groups to keep written notes of their points.
7. Then ask three groups representing different PMI approaches (one P, one M, one I) to join together to make a larger group. Give these larger groups a copy of the worksheet provided.
8. This larger group then looks at all the issues that have been raised and completes the worksheet, listing the good points, the bad points, and the interesting points they have identified.
9. Ask students to put the worksheets up on the walls for all students to read.
10. Facilitate a class discussion where students are encouraged to think more broadly about the topic and to highlight which of the interesting points raised deserve more attention.
11. Finally, ask which students have changed their opinion and why. Which students have not and why not? How flexible are students in terms of changing their minds?

Extension

The material developed in the activity can be used as the basis of a written assignment. Students can use the tables to defend or oppose the proposition. Another approach might be to have the students explore the proposition focusing on interesting ideas that have been raised. Another activity might be to ask groups to come up with their own propositions, which other groups in the class could then consider.

Teacher Reflection

One of the points that de Bono makes is that people are very quick to form an opinion, quite often without having given much thought to

55

From Implications to Application

the matter. They rely on first impressions, bias, or traditional views. He argues that quite often, intelligent people are the worst offenders, and because they are smart, they can come up with reasons to defend points of view they haven't really considered deeply.

1. Are you guilty of forming opinions too quickly? Has this ever been a problem?
2. Do you typically make quick professional decisions?
3. Should you slow down? Is there time to slow down?
4. Can you tell a story of a time when a decision you made at school was too late?
5. Can you think of a professional decision you have made in the past that you would make quite differently now?

Materials

Example of propositions:

- *Only one kind of car should be manufactured worldwide.*
- *University students should be paid a wage while they are studying.*
- *All countries should make English compulsory from the first year of school.*
- *Cancer treatments should be supplied free of charge to all citizens of my country.*

Let's take a closer look at: *Only one kind of car should be manufactured worldwide.*

Plus	Minus	Interesting
Cars could be built very cheaply.	Making cars even more affordable would result in more congestion and pollution.	Would people find other ways to make their cars different?

From Implications to Application

Plus	Minus	Interesting
More people would be able to afford cars.	Such a move would discourage technological developments.	Would more or fewer people use public transport?
The speed at which cars travel could be controlled, resulting in fewer accidents.	Thousands of jobs would be lost in car factories around the world.	Would the roads be safer if we all drove the same cars?
High standard of safety features would be built into every car.	People would be denied freedom of choice.	Would car racing as a sport still exist?
Cars would no longer be status symbols.	Cars give people a great deal of pleasure— they would be denied this pleasure.	Would we extend this idea to motorbikes and scooters?
Cars could be designed to be more environmentally friendly.	If people lost interest in their cars they would not bother to maintain them properly.	Would people become more interested in things such as boats and bicycles?

Combined group worksheet

Proposition:		
Plus	Minus	Interesting

(Continued)

57

From Implications to Application

(Continued)

Proposition:		
Plus	**Minus**	**Interesting**

Activity 8: The Genders of Objects

Introduction

Some languages mark certain grammatical items with gender. English does not do this. In this activity, students consider a number of English nouns and compare their perceptions of the nouns depending on whether they have been identified as masculine or feminine. Students work in groups to do this, and then whole-class discussion follows on how our gendered identities are marked or signalled and how sometimes gendered identities can be imposed on people and things.

Aim:	- To review grammatical gender
	- To consider perceptions of gender in objects
	- To critically examine imposed gendered identities
Level:	Intermediate
Time:	40 minutes
Materials:	Task sheets A and B and dictionaries for use in class. Students could use online dictionaries on their smart phones or tablets.

From Implications to Application

Preparation: Prepare basic information about grammatical gender in languages, such as Spanish marking nouns grammatically for gender.

Language practice	
Skills?	speaking, listening
What?	adjectives, descriptive vocabulary and phrases, discussing different perceptions, comparing
How?	whole group discussion, describing objects in groups, comparing in groups

Procedure

1. Briefly compare the fact that the English language does not ascribe gender to all nouns and that some languages do. Provide some examples such as *el arbor* (the tree, in Spanish, masculine).
2. On the board write the word *table*. Ask students to imagine that nouns in English have a gender, and *table* is a masculine noun. Ask them to suggest adjectives to describe table (e.g., heavy, strong, large, useful). According to level, more sophisticated adjective phrases could be suggested, such as 'a heavy piece of furniture'.
3. Organize students in an equal number of small groups. Label half the groups A and half B.
4. Distribute Task Sheets A and B. The groups suggest adjectives or adjective phrases to fill in the empty boxes (as in 2). They can use dictionaries to do this. Give a limited time, such as 10 minutes.
5. Join each A group with a B group to compare the suggestions and to discuss:

   Did we use similar adjectives for each noun (when the noun was given as 'masculine' compared with 'feminine')?

6. Review findings from the groups and list suggested adjectives on the board. Make two columns on the board: adjectives used for

59

From Implications to Application

masculine objects and adjectives used for feminine objects. Identify any trends in adjectives in relation to gender.

7. Use findings and adjectives on the board as a point of departure for discussion of how we identify our own gendered identities by the language we use and how sometimes gendered identities can be *imposed* on people and things. Ask questions such as:

- How does the use of certain words that reflect gender, such as *boy* or *girl*, make you feel when they are used about you?
- How do you prefer to talk about yourself when using gendered words?
- Why are masculine objects and male people generally seen as strong?
- Where do these ideas come from?
- Do you feel people sometimes see you in a particular way because of your gender?
- Would you like this to be different? What should change?

Teacher Reflection

Consider how you respond to male and female students? Does their gender in any way impact on how you perceive and respond to them? Think of the students in your classes and complete the following phrases with *boy*, *girl*, *man*, or *woman*:

1. naughty _____.
2. silly _____
3. grumpy old _____
4. complaining old _____
5. talkative _____
6. cheeky _____
7. clever _____
8. charming _____

60

Materials

Task Sheet A

	Adjective or adjective phrase
bridge (masculine)	
sun (masculine)	
moon (feminine)	
cloud (feminine)	
basket (masculine)	
boat (feminine)	

Task Sheet B

	Adjective or adjective phrase
bridge (feminine)	
sun (feminine)	
moon (masculine)	
cloud (masculine)	
basket (feminine)	
boat (masculine)	

Activity 9: Food and Identity

Introduction

This activity focuses on the topic of food and identity and the way in which the two are closely linked. Our practices around the foods that we eat play an important part in how we identify ourselves and how our identities become evident to others. In this activity, students discuss the differences between formal and informal writing, practice summarizing, and work out the meanings of words from their context.

From Implications to Application

Aim:	- To point out differences between formal and informal language
	- To practice summarizing
	- To show students they can work out what a word means from the context
	- To reflect on the students' cultural practices regarding food
Level:	Intermediate
Time:	60 minutes (perhaps longer over two lessons)
Materials:	A worksheet with two tasks is provided.
Preparation:	Prepare copies of the worksheet for each student.

Language practice

Skills?	multiple skills, vocabulary
What?	differentiating between formal and informal writing, summarizing, working out the meaning of words from the context, sharing cultural experiences
How?	reading formal and informal texts individually, summarizing and formalizing an informal text individually, discussing food and identity as a whole class and in groups

Procedure

Part 1

1. This first part of this lesson aims to show students the difference between formal and informal language and how different vocabulary choices are employed to do this.
2. Hand out the worksheets and ask students to read Task 1.
3. Ask them to identify some of the words or phrases that they think are informal (e.g., a lot of, they just). Discuss with them more formal alternatives to these words.
4. Ask students to find instances where Raj has repeated himself. Point out to them that while it is common to use repetition in

62

From Implications to Application

spoken language in formal written language, this is not a good idea.

5. Discuss summarizing with students. Tell them a summary is a shortened version of the original passage. It seeks to capture the main points as succinctly as possible. It is usually written in formal language.

6. Ask students to complete Task 1 on the worksheet individually.

7. When the class has completed this work, discuss their answers with them.

8. Point out to them that they have changed informal words into more formal ones. One of the difficulties students experience in reading formal English is that they are often unfamiliar with the vocabulary used.

Part 2

9. The second part of the activity requires students to work out the meanings of words from their context.

10. Ask students to read the passage in Task 2, which contains more formal vocabulary, and then to answer the questions.

11. Bring them back together to discuss the answers as a class.

12. At this stage you can point out to students that most of them were probably able to come up with the right answers even though they might not have understood all the words in the passage. They used the context of the passage to help them. You can stress to them that this is a very important skill.

13. The students have worked hard on their own. End the lesson by facilitating a discussion on the different types of food that are eaten around the world. Raj says that he eats differently now that he lives in Canada. What are the big changes he has made to his diet?

14. If the students in your class are drawn from other countries, ask them to discuss the following in groups:

   a. What changes have you made to your diet?
   b. Are there foods that you miss?
   c. Can you find them in the country you now live in?

63

From Implications to Application

    d.   Do you try to eat as you did back home?

    e.   If you meet up with people who share your ethnicity, are there particular foods that you cook?

15. If the students are in their own country, ask them to discuss the following in groups:

    a.   What are the foods that you think are particularly special to your country?

    b.   If you were entertaining people from other countries, what dishes would you serve to them?

    c.   Why do you think these dishes are special?

    d.   Do you eat differently from the way your parents ate?

16. If the class is made up of students from both groups, you might want to divide them as suggested earlier, or perhaps it might be more interesting to have mixed groups.

Extension

For more advanced groups, you might select a passage with more difficult words, or you might ask students to come up with their own definitions of the words. You could also increase the difficulty of the passage you ask the students to summarize.

Elementary students could be given a passage with easier words, or the teacher could work through the exercise with them. Instead of summarizing a passage, they could be asked to identify where repetition takes place. They could also be asked to supply more formal synonyms for a few words.

Students from all ability levels might enjoy describing a dish they find particularly tasty. They could be asked to prepare a recipe in such a way that a person not familiar with the particular culture would be able to follow. Students could also be asked to do an internet search for items in the menu that are not readily available around the world and find other food items that could substitute for the original ingredients.

From Implications to Application

Teacher Reflection

What role does food play in celebrations and other social gatherings in your professional institution?

1. On what occasions is food consumed (e.g., meetings, birthday celebrations)? Any others?
2. Who brings the food? Who pays for it?
3. Who eats the most?
4. Who doesn't usually eat anything?
5. Are dietary restrictions considered?
6. Are there favorite dishes amongst the teachers? What are they?
7. How do you 'behave' around food at these social gatherings?

Consider how social practices involving food in your institution project the identities of those who gather to eat and enjoy it.

Materials

Worksheet

Task 1

These are the words of Raj, who moved to Canada from Punjab:

> Here in Canada, eating bread is very common. I worked in the mill for three months and saw that some people do not eat roti here; they just eat bread, so even I started eating bread. I eat a lot of meat here. Here we live in the city, and everything is available; there we used to live in the village, and everything is not available in the villages. So we have to drive 10 km to the city to buy meat. But even the people in the cities do not eat meat very often. They also cook meat just once in a while. In Punjab people eat less meat. (110 words)

Summarize Raj's statement in your own words. Raj repeats himself a few times. When you are summarizing, try to give the main idea of a piece of writing as briefly as you can. Try to rewrite the information in this

65

From Implications to Application

passage in less than 60 words. Because the passage is giving the actual words that Raj used, the language is informal. In your summary, try to use more formal English.

Task 2

Read the passage and then find the words that match the definitions below it:

> Food has long been understood as an important marker of cultural identity. The foodstuffs that go into a person's diet, the recipes that are used to cook these foods, and the ways in which they are eaten are some of the most obvious signs that someone belongs to a specific ethnic group. For migrants living far from their country of origin, the continued consumption of food from their own country can be an important way to maintain a connection to that country. Food practices play an important role in people's construction of their identity.

[Adapted from: Chapman, G., & Beagan, B. (2013). Food practices and transnational identities. *Food, Culture & Society*, *16*, 367–386.]

Find words in the passage that match these definitions:

a. the action of linking one thing with another
b. the action of eating or drinking something
c. enable a situation to continue
d. relating to national and cultural origins
e. clearly defined or identified
f. easily perceived or understood

Activity 10: Author Presence

Introduction

In academic writing, the presence of the author is marked by use of first person or masked by use of third person. In this activity, the students consider how this is done in samples of academic writing, including their own.

66

From Implications to Application

Aim:	- To consider how writers construct identities in academic writing
	- To reflect on personal preferences for referring to self as author
Level:	Intermediate
Time:	50 minutes
Materials:	Samples of student academic writing
Preparation:	- Find two samples of student-level academic writing for use as examples for your class.
	- In the sample texts, identify any references to the writer as an individual by highlighting or underlining uses of personal pronouns (*I, my*) that signal opinions or personal agency of the writer.
	- Also identify and highlight places where opinions or agency are masked by third-person formulations, such as *It is clear that, It seems that*, or *It is important to note*.
	- Use text parts rather than the entire text if the samples are long.
	- Prepare the two samples for use in class (clean photocopies and marked up copies).
	- Ask students to bring to class an essay or report they have written (any type of academic writing).

Language practice	
Skills?	writing, reading
What?	giving opinions, analyzing own writing, reporting
How?	whole-class question and answer, independent reading

Procedure

1. Write the following on the board:

   Sample A: Student essay on 'The impact of social media'

67

From Implications to Application

- *It is believed that social media changes the way people interact.*
- *I believe social media changes the way people interact.*

Sample B: Student report of the procedures she used in her research

- *I examined the data and identified two patterns.*
- *The data was examined, and two patterns were identified.*

2. Ask students the following questions in relation to samples A and B:

Sample A

Do the sentences refer to the same opinion?
Why do writers refer to opinions as their own or try to avoid this?

Sample B

Do the sentences report the same information?
Why do writers refer to themselves as agents or try to avoid this?
Explain that academic writers have choices. They can refer to themselves as individuals with opinions and agency, or they can mask their opinions and agency through the use of third-person formulations.

3. Show students one of the sample texts you prepared in advance. Discuss examples of overt references to the author and examples of where opinions and agency are masked behind third-person formulations.
4. Give students the other sample text and ask them to identify overt references to the authors and examples of opinions and agency masked behind third-person formulations.
5. Review and ask students to compare the two samples:
    Was the author's presence more obvious in one of the samples?

68

From Implications to Application

6. Ask students whether they generally try to mask opinions and agency in their own academic writing. (This question asks them what they think they do in their writing.)
7. Students examine the sample of their writing they brought to class. They underline instances when they referred to themselves as individuals with opinions and agency and when they masked their opinions and agency through the use of third-person formulations. (This activity requires students to examine what they do in an example of their writing practice.)
8. Ask students what they found when they examined their writing. On reflection, would they make any changes to the extent they referred to themselves as individuals with opinions and agency or masked their opinions and agency?

Extension

Students can do a more extensive review of their writing. They can examine multiple texts they have written.

For an advanced class, students could examine professional academic writing, such as parts of articles or book chapters. They identify the range of third-person formulations used and try to extend their linguistic repertoire.

Teacher Reflection

Reflect on the following questions:

1. To what extent do you refer to yourself personally when you give opinions in classroom interaction? How obvious is your presence in what you say?
2. How do you respond to your students' writing? Do you expect or encourage them to play up or play down their presence?

From Implications to Application

Activity 11: Chickens in Cages

Introduction

Students' decisions about what they eat and do not eat might simply be a matter of what they enjoy, but increasingly people are becoming more aware of environmental and ethical concerns relating to the way their food is produced. What we believe to be the right way to behave is very much part of our identity. For example, certain religions forbid their followers from consuming certain foods. This activity asks students to identify the advantages and disadvantages of a particular farming activity, namely farming chickens in cages. The activity includes rewriting formal English in a more accessible way and an exercise to develop students' vocabulary.

Aim:	- To identify arguments for and against a farming practice
	- To identify differences between formal and informal writing (vocabulary and grammar)
Level:	Advanced
Time:	60 minutes
Materials:	A worksheet that can be used individually or in groups
Preparation:	Prepare copies of the worksheet provided for each student.

Language practice	
Skills?	speaking, writing
What?	identifying points for and against in an argument, rewriting formal language in an informal way
How?	whole-class discussion, completing worksheets individually or in groups

70

From Implications to Application

Procedure

1. Start a discussion with the class about the issues outlined in the introduction. Use some of these questions:

   - What do they think about animal rights?
   - Are there students in the class who do not eat meat?
   - Do they choose not to eat meat because of religious or environmental concerns or because they are worried about the wellbeing of farmed animals?
   - How important are their beliefs to them?

2. Then give each student a copy of the worksheet.
3. Ask them to read the statements and complete the table. This activity can be done in small groups or individually.
4. After the worksheet has been completed, allow students to discuss which argument they thought was the strongest. Do they necessarily agree with this argument?
5. Ask them to reflect on what their opinion says about themselves (they can do this silently).
6. Call for whole-class feedback when they have completed their discussion and silent reflection.
7. Draw the students' attention to the way in which the given information is written. It is very formal. Discuss why that author chose to write in this way.

Extension

These worksheets could form the basis of other activities. Ask students to file them carefully. Students could identify a controversial topic to explore (e.g., legalizing the sale of marijuana). Students could search for advantages and disadvantages of implementing ideas like this, and then based on the evidence they have found, form their own opinions (What do their opinions say about who they are?). Justifying these opinions could be done in classroom debates or formal essays or informal writing assignments. Students could also be asked to reflect on their own personal beliefs. If they believe legalizing marijuana, for instance, is wrong, would they make

From Implications to Application

exceptions for people with medical conditions? What about people who have mental health issues? Are there degrees of 'wrongness'?

Teacher Reflection

Topics such as legalizing marijuana or caging chickens are often difficult to discuss, not only because of the controversial content but also because people may be disinclined to share their personal opinions, revealing their backgrounds and world-views in the process. Think about your language classes:

1. Do you regularly facilitate the exploration of topics such as these in class?
2. If you do, do you tend to favor material that justifies your perspective?
3. Are students given opportunities to consider their views on these matters?
4. How engaged in discussions do students become?
5. Which topics work best (and which have failed) to generate productive discussion?

Materials

Worksheet (Group or Individual)

Read the information provided and then decide whether each point made is in favor of keeping caged hens or in favor of keeping uncaged hens.

1. Keeping hens in cages means that they are separated from their feces. Therefore, infections cannot be spread by feces.
2. Because there is less dust in cages than in other types of accommodation for hens, they are less likely to suffer from respiratory diseases.
3. Hens kept in cages have less lower limb bone strength than birds that are not caged.
4. Fowls prefer to live in groups with a dominant male and 4 to 12 females. This grouping is more closely reflected in the caged system than in the non-caged system.

From Implications to Application

5. To ensure the welfare of the birds, inspection is a requirement. Inspecting caged birds is more time consuming that inspecting uncaged hens.
6. The costs associated with the management of uncaged birds are considerably higher than their caged counterparts.
7. Uncaged birds, on the whole, produce a greater quantity of eggs than those in cages.
8. Caged hens are unable to find and make their own nests. Their inability to follow their natural instincts leads to frustration and stress.
9. Uncaged hens have greater freedom of movement that caged birds. Unhampered movement leads to better health and greater egg production.

[Information from: Duncan, I. (2001). The pros and cons of cages. *Worlds Poultry Science Journal*, *57*, 389–390.]

Complete the table below. Keep the reasons short and use your own words as far as possible. One advantage and one disadvantage have been filled in to show you what to do.

Advantages to keeping hens in cages	Disadvantages to keeping hens in cages
Hens in cages live in the kind of groups they like.	Uncaged birds are healthier and happier than caged birds because uncaged birds can move around freely.

The language employed in the worksheet is very formal because it has been taken from an academic journal article. Academic writing is always

73

From Implications to Application

formal and that can mean that it is not always easy to understand. Look at the table below. There is a list of words or phrases that have been taken from the worksheet. Read them in the context of the passage. Can you find other words or phrases that could be used that would be easier to understand?

Formal language	Informal language
feces	
lower limb	
dominant	
considerably	
natural instincts	
unhampered	
counterparts	

Look at the following sentences. How could you rewrite them to make the text easier to read?

Formal language	Informal language
To ensure the welfare of the birds, inspection is a requirement.	
The costs associated with the management of uncaged birds are considerably higher than their caged counterparts.	
Uncaged birds, on the whole, produce a greater quantity of eggs than those in cages.	

74

From Implications to Application

Activity 12: My Ideal Holiday

Introduction

The kinds of holidays that people enjoy vary greatly. What we enjoy is closely linked to our likes and dislikes, the kinds of people we like to meet, the food we like to eat, sights we like to see. In other words, our identities. Some of us are thrill seekers who enjoy holidays with an element of danger, while others like nothing more than to relax on a beautiful beach. In this activity, students critique different categories of travellers. They then select a category that suits them and in groups work out their ideal holiday.

Aim:	- To think about the kind of travel students enjoy
	- To analyze why this travel appeals to them
	- To conceptualize their ideal holiday
	- To cooperate within a group to develop a description of an ideal trip
Level:	Advanced
Time:	60 minutes
Materials:	A worksheet is provided.
Preparation:	- Think about what kind of a tourist you are. Where would your ideal holiday be, and why would you choose this destination?
	- Make copies of the worksheet provided for each student.

Language practice	
Skills?	speaking, writing, critical thinking
What?	analyzing preferences, justifying choices, writing in groups
How?	whole-class discussion, working in groups, collaborative writing

From Implications to Application

Procedure

1. Start a class discussion about overseas travel. Millions of people now enjoy overseas travel. Statistics show that in 2017, there were 1.32 billion tourist arrivals at different airports around the world. While Europe and the Americas remain the most popular destinations, with France heading the list of most visited countries, other destinations such as Iceland, Vietnam, and Uruguay are increasing in popularity. In addition, there are many new ways to spend a holiday, so there is growing interest in categorizing tourists. This is done to help these tourists choose a holiday they feel is right for them.
2. Give students an opportunity to talk about (overseas) trips they might have taken.
3. Ask students to get into groups of three or four students and hand out the worksheet, one for each student.
4. Ask them to look at the categories listed under A. What do they think of the categories and their descriptions? Encourage them to make changes to the categories on the worksheet and add new ones if they feel they can be improved. They might think that two different categories would be better listed as one.
5. When the groups have completed the task in Section A, bring the class together and, working with the students, come up with a revised list of categories.
6. Ask each student to pick a category that they believe suits them (Section B on the worksheet).
7. After they have selected a category ask them to form groups of three or four with students who chose the same category.
8. Each group then brainstorms what they consider to be an ideal holiday for people in that category (see questions in Section C of the worksheet). Tell them that they can choose up to three different destinations. The holiday should be about three weeks long.
9. The groups must then write a description of their ideal holiday. Students could use the internet to find out about the types of holidays that are available.

From Implications to Application

Extension

This particular activity does not ask students to investigate factors such as price. However, in another lesson, students could fill in the details about their dream trip. They could work out travel and accommodation expenses, the cost of hiring equipment such as bicycles, and issues around visas. Less advanced students could be given brochures about overseas trips and asked to select which one they would choose and explain why.

Teacher Reflection

Think about any work-related travel you do—for example, to meetings, professional development workshops, conferences. Some of these might take you out of your district, out of town, or even out of the country.

1. How do you project your professional identity when you travel? What sort of teacher are you as a professional traveler?
2. Do any of the following apply to you?
   a. gossip about your colleagues
   b. complain about your institution
   c. boost the reputation of your school
   d. try to recruit teachers or students
   e. look for interesting and useful teaching materials to purchase
   f. present your research or teaching ideas
   g. envy professionals in the visited location
   h. keep an eye out for other jobs
   i. like to travel with colleagues from your school or prefer to travel alone
   j. always aim to learn as much as possible

From Implications to Application

Materials

Worksheet

A. Categories of Tourists

1. *Thrill seeker*—Your ideal holiday might be surfing huge waves in Hawaii or skiing difficult ski runs in Canada. You like your holidays to have an element of danger. Perhaps you would like the opportunity to learn a new sport like scuba diving.
2. *Culture buff*—You are particularly interested in the cultural achievements in other countries. You want to see beautiful artwork and buildings. You enjoy visiting museums.
3. *Active traveler*—You like to be active and enjoy cycling and hiking in your destination country.
4. *Hands-on traveler*—You like learning new skills or improving existing ones. You would like to join a painting course or cookery class, preferably in a new exciting destination.
5. *Nature lover*—Your interest is in natural beauty and wildlife. You would like to travel to the Amazon or the Antarctic or African game reserves.
6. *Relaxed visitor*—You want to go somewhere beautiful and peaceful where you can relax and unwind. Perhaps you enjoy spas and massages. You don't want an active holiday.
7. *A people person*—You want to know how other people live. You would like an opportunity to experience local life, perhaps live with a family or visit small villages off the tourist track.

What do you think of these categories? Would you add others? Do you think some of the categories above are not good descriptions? Do you think some should be merged?

B. What Kind of Tourist Are You?

C. Group Work

You have all identified with a particular kind of tourist. Work together to write collectively a description of your ideal holiday. The questions below will give you some ideas. This description should be about 500 words in

From Implications to Application

length. All members of your group may not personally agree with every aspect of the description because this is a collective description. So this will be an ideal holiday for your group.

1. What will the main focus of your holiday be?
2. What is/are the destination(s) you will visit?
3. What do you plan to do there?
4. Why have you chosen this/these destination(s)? Why are they important to you?
5. How long will you spend there?
6. What do you hope will be the outcome of your holiday?
7. What do you think the highlights will be?
8. How do these holidays reflect who you are as a person?

C. Projecting Identities

Table 2.3 Projecting identities: Activity titles and aims

Activity	Title	Aims
Activity 13	Introducing Ourselves	• To listen for information in recordings of people introducing themselves • To record their findings on a listening task sheet • To role play personal introductions • To consider how each of us is a collection of identities
Activity 14	What's in a Name?	• To talk and write about the importance of names • To write short paragraphs • To practice using conjunctions • To join two short paragraphs to form a longer paragraph

(*Continued*)

79

Table 2.3 (Continued)

Activity	Title	Aims
Activity 15	Gay Men Playing Rugby	• To prepare for a debate by identifying relevant adjectives • To express an opinion by developing an argument • To engage in a debate • To write reflective notes summarizing the debate
Activity 16	Relationships and Age	• To listen to a song and write down vocabulary items from the song • To collaborate in pairs to write a dialogue • To perform the dialogue in front of the class • To discuss the nature of the relationship between the older and younger speakers as portrayed in the dialogues
Activity 17	The Clothes We Wear	• To read a short story and select vocabulary items • To collaborate in groups to write a poem • To read the poem aloud to the class • To discuss the relationship between the clothes we wear and our identities
Activity 18	Why Is Facebook So Popular?	• To consider and evaluate social media use • To list explanations according to which are most plausible • To reflect on how Facebook users project their identities online • To defend choice in small group, inter-group, and whole-class arrangements

Activity	Title	Aims
Activity 19	Idiomatic Language	• To promote the understanding and use of idiomatic English • To encourage appreciation of the idioms in students' first languages • To understand the difference between the literal and figurative meaning of words
Activity 20	Make Your Own Cartoon	• To understand and practice direct and indirect speech • To examine the changes that are made when direct speech is reported • To tell a joke or story in direct speech • To retell the joke or story in indirect speech
Activity 21	There's a Little Bit of Good in Everyone	• To understand and define 'good' and 'bad' personality traits • To challenge accepted stereotypes • To consider the consequences of projecting personality traits
Activity 22	Proverbs and You	• To understanding English proverbs • To link proverbs to their meanings • To illustrate the meaning of a proverb by referring to something that has happened in one's life • To write a paragraph about a life experience

(*Continued*)

From Implications to Application

Table 2.3 (Continued)

Activity	Title	Aims
Activity 23	Justifying Your Opinion	• To justify an opinion • To identify differences between formal and informal writing (vocabulary and syntax) • To summarize arguments succinctly • To rewrite formal arguments informally • To write persuasively using available evidence
Activity 24	Pictures at an Exhibition	• To develop a project that involves independent and group research • To collect sources of information from outside the classroom • To search the internet • To present a curated exhibition

Activity 13: Introducing Ourselves

Introduction

When people meet someone for the first time, their personal introductions include information that they want to share—information that is appropriate for the circumstances, including who the interlocutor is. They can draw on their multiple identities selectively when introducing themselves. After first listening to recorded samples of people doing introductions, this activity asks students to consider the kinds of information they would share when introducing themselves and in what order.

Aim: -   To listen for information in recordings of people introducing themselves

From Implications to Application

	- To record their findings on a listening task sheet
	- To role play personal introductions
	- To consider how each of us is a collection of identities
Level:	Elementary
Time:	60 minutes
Materials:	Audio recordings of teacher introductions and worksheet for listening task (see Materials)
Preparation:	- Ask about four teachers or administrators in your school to imagine that they are introducing themselves (monologue) to a new teacher in the school. They can talk (briefly for a minute or two) about work, age, religion, first language(s), and cultural or ethnic background. They do not need to include all these topics or to talk about the topics in this order, and they can include additional topics. Make audio recordings of their introductions.
	- Prepare copies of the Listening Task Sheet. Identify any specific linguistic expressions in the recordings to focus on in the lesson.

Language practice	
Skills?	listening, speaking, writing
What?	listening for information in audio-recordings, taking written notes, reporting findings orally, role playing oral introductions
How?	whole-class instruction, working in pairs, whole class question and answer

Procedure

1. On the board, write: 'The kinds of information we give when we introduce ourselves'. Ask students to suggest kinds of information.
2. Write their suggestions on the board, such as age, occupation, and first language background.

From Implications to Application

3. Tell the students to listen to recordings of two teachers or administrators introducing themselves to a new teacher in the school. The students listen and check which kinds of information the teachers included. They could take notes (keywords and phrases) to help them recall what they heard.
4. Ask students for their answers. Review and point out that the teachers did or did not include the same kinds of information or use the same order of information as you wrote earlier on the board.
5. Hand out copies of the Listening Task.
6. Students listen to the remaining (two or three) recordings and make notes in the empty boxes.
7. Ask students to review their answers in pairs.
8. Then all come together to review answers. Lead discussion on the kinds of information included and the order of information. Write these on the board.
9. Students listen to the recordings again. This time, they note any additional details and/or linguistic expressions specific to personal introductions (e.g., *"I come from," I haven't always been," "and then I"*) in the boxes.
10. Review additional details and provide a language focus by recording a selection of the linguistic expressions on the board. Ask students to write these down in their notebooks for later revision.
11. Tell students that they are going to introduce themselves to others in the class, perhaps those whom they do not know well. They need to give their name but can only give four other kinds of information. Students prepare by writing down the kinds of information they will give, possible expressions they will use, and the order of information.
12. Students then mix and mingle introducing themselves to class members they do not know well.
13. After all students have had a few turns introducing themselves, review the activity using questions such as:

    - Did everyone include age? Why or why not?
    - How many people included religion?

84

From Implications to Application

- Was it easy or difficult to choose the kinds of information you offered?
- What did you most want people to know about you?
- What did you talk about first and second? Why in this order?

14. End the activity by discussing with students how we project our identities in oral interactions, especially in personal introductions. You could ask them if they believe that first impressions matter!

Extension

As an extension in a later writing activity, explore how introductions vary in different settings. Tell students that they are going to post written introductions of themselves on two (hypothetical) websites (perhaps 50–75 words).

- The first website is for English-language learners wanting to connect with others from the same language and/or cultural background who are learning English.
- The second website is for English-language learners wanting to connect with people from different first language and/or cultural backgrounds who are learning English.
- What would they include in their introductions?

Teacher Reflection

Imagine you are at a professional development workshop for language teachers in your district. There will be teachers there from other schools. They will also be language teachers. When you meet during the first coffee break, they will probably want to know who you are, what you teach, and who your students are—and a lot more besides.

Over a cup of coffee, how would you introduce yourself to those teachers?

From Implications to Application

Materials

Listening Task Sheet

Example

Teacher: Anne
Kinds of information and selected details
Age: late 30s English teacher, 4+ years ("*I haven't always been an English teacher, though*") First language: English Family/cultural background: English mother and Australian father—grew up in Sydney Mother, a boy ("coming up to his second birthday")

Teacher:
Kinds of information and selected details:

Activity 14: What's in a Name?

Introduction

In this activity, students consider the importance of names and how they reflect our identity. Students write a short paragraph explaining the various names or nicknames they answer to.

Aim:
- To talk and write about the importance of names
- To write short paragraphs
- To practice using conjunctions

86

From Implications to Application

- To join two short paragraphs to form a longer paragraph

Level: Elementary

Time: 60 minutes

Materials: A worksheet provided; examples of names and their meanings

Preparation: Find examples of first names that will be familiar to some of your students.

Language practice	
Skills?	speaking, writing, reading aloud
What?	completing sentences giving reasons, joining two paragraphs, using conjunctions
How?	whole-class discussion, completing worksheets individually, reading aloud paragraphs to the class

Procedure

1. Discuss the different names by which we are known with the class. Most of us answer to different names in different contexts. For example, you might be Mr. or Ms. + last name to your students but Pete or Nelly to your friends. Sometimes the names on our birth certificates are not the ones that we use commonly. For various reasons, we may use different names that were officially given to us.

2. Give the students examples. Queen Elizabeth II is affectionately known as Lilibet because she couldn't pronounce her own name when she was small. Nelson Mandela wasn't called Nelson by his family. They called him Rolihlahla, which means troublemaker. On his first day of school, his teacher said he would be known as Nelson probably because it was easier for white people to pronounce. Try to find examples of prominent figures with whom your students are familiar.

3. Hand out the worksheet, one to each student, and ask them to consider the given example in Part A (or another one that you create).

87

From Implications to Application

Point out to them that it is quite likely that different people will be called different names depending on who is addressing them.

4. Ask students to complete the Part A.

5. When students have completed Part A, talk about the different reasons parents have for the names they choose for their children. Sometimes there is a traditional reason for a name; a boy might be named after his father or grandfather, while a girl might be named after her mother or grandmother. Parents might choose a name because of its meaning.

6. Then ask students to write a short paragraph about why they were given their first names and what they mean (Part B of the worksheet). They could start the paragraph:

   a. I was named _____ because _____. My name means _____.

7. The students could then join the two short paragraphs into one longer one.

8. The students take turns reading their paragraphs out to the class.

Extension/Variation

Sometimes people choose to be known by different names. Chinese students might use Western names. Perhaps some of your students have chosen different names for themselves. If they have never thought about another name for themselves, ask them to think about it now. Put students in groups and ask them to discuss the following:

- If you have chosen to use another name, what is it, and why did you choose this name? Where do you use it?
- If you haven't chosen to use another name, think about a name you might choose. Why would you choose this name? Can you think of where you might use this name?

Then ask each student to list the various reasons people gave for choosing names. What do they think about these reasons?

88

From Implications to Application

Teacher Reflection

Our names are an integral part of our identities. Following are some questions to prompt reflection on names in your life as a teacher.

1. Remembering and using your students' names demonstrates an interest in your students. Do you learn and remember all your students' names?
2. Do you know how to pronounce their names? Why do you think it is a good idea to do so?
3. Do you use your students' preferred names? Do you know if they have a preferred name?
4. To what extent do you integrate the use of students' names in your classroom talk?
5. What do your students call *you*?

Material

Worksheet

Part A

Look at this example and then complete the sentences below about yourself.

My name is Patricia, **but** my friends call me Pat. My grandparents call me Tricia, **and** my swimming coach calls me Patty. My parents always call me Patricia. I like it best **when** people call me Pat. I like Pat or Patty **because** I don't like the sound of Patricia and **because** Patricia always sounds as if people are cross with me!

My name is _____, **but** my friends/classmates/teacher call/s me _____. My parents/ mother/father/ grandparents call/s me _____, **and** my other family members call me_____. I like it best **when** people call me _____ **because** _____.

89

From Implications to Application

Part B

I was named _____ because _____. My name means _____.

Activity 15: Gay Men Playing Rugby

Introduction

This activity requires students to consider whether gay men do play rugby and to reflect on reasons for their and their classmate's opinions. For students unfamiliar with rugby, you will describe the sport, or they can watch a YouTube video showing excerpts of rugby in action. The activity gives the students the opportunity to confront their own and others' images of contact sports and how they are compatible with their images of homosexual men. The activity makes the connection between ideas about a particular sport and one's perceptions of the identities of the people who play that sport.

Aim:	- To prepare for a debate by identifying relevant adjectives
	- To express an opinion by developing an argument
	- To engage in a debate
	- To write reflective notes summarizing the debate
Level:	Intermediate
Time:	60 minutes
Materials:	YouTube videos, notebook for students, student tablets or smart phones
Preparation:	- Have available the two YouTube video clips or ask students to bring their tablets or smart phones to class.
	- Watch the videos or prepare some notes on the characteristics of rugby.
	- Prepare a working list of possible reasons students might give to support or not support their opinions of gay men playing rugby.

90

From Implications to Application

Language practice	
Skills?	writing, speaking, listening, critical thinking
What?	expressing an opinion, developing an argument, comparing, negative and positive adjectives
How?	independent writing, sharing in pairs, reading aloud to whole class, informal debating, silent reflection

Procedure

1. Ask students who are familiar with the game of rugby to describe collaboratively the game to the rest of the class.
2. Summarize and elaborate on the students' description or start from the beginning if none of them is familiar with rugby. Describe the game to the students. Show students the following YouTube video clips (or search 'what is rugby' on YouTube), or they can access it on their mobile phones:

   www.youtube.com/watch?v=-FSMZza9oWE
   www.youtube.com/watch?v=MDYMUf-Q5vY

3. Ask students to write down in their notebooks five adjectives that describe their impressions of rugby.
4. When they have finished, in pairs students share their list of adjectives with each other. Ask the students to identify positive (e.g., beautiful, flowing, strategic, exciting) and negative (e.g., violent, dangerous, rough) adjectives.
5. Ask for volunteers to read out to the whole class their list of positive and negative adjectives. Write a selection of these on the whiteboard.
6. Introduce the word 'masculine' to the class and highlight synonyms associated with this word. Ask students to select words from the list on the whiteboard that reflect masculinity (circle those words), or a masculine identity.
7. Inform students that very few professional rugby players have 'come out' as gay. Give the students two to three minutes in silence to reflect on why this might be the case.

From Implications to Application

8. Prepare for an informal debate: Divide the class into two groups.
9. One group will argue, *Gay men play rugby*, and the other group will argue, *Gay men do not play rugby*.
10. Give the groups five minutes to consider and prepare their argument. Suggest they list four or five reasons and consult the list of adjectives on the whiteboard to generate ideas.
11. Conduct the informal debate, giving each side the opportunity to state one reason to support their argument, and then giving the other side the opportunity to oppose their reason. Work through several points in turn from each side. Aim to distribute speaking opportunities among the students.
12. End the lesson by giving the students five minutes to write in their notebooks reflective comments that summarize for them the main arguments from both sides. (These notes could be used for a later composition writing activity.)
13. At the start of the next class, after students have had some time to digest the content of the debate (which might affect some students personally), summarize the arguments put forward by the students. Relate the discussion to identity, particularly the decisions people make about projecting their identities to others.

Teacher Reflection

1. What about gay and lesbian teachers? Consider your institution. How gay friendly is it?
   a. Are there any gay or lesbian teachers in your institution?
   b. Are you aware of any institutional support for them?
   c. Does their sexuality affect their teaching practice in any way?
2. How could your institution be more gay friendly?
   a. Are there any sexuality-related policies in place?
   b. Have you ever noticed any student reaction to gay faculty? What did you think about their reaction, and did you do anything about it?

From Implications to Application

Activity 16: Relationships and Age

Introduction

In this activity, students will write a dialogue between an older and a younger person in pairs. Drawing on vocabulary heard in a song, students will write and then perform the dialogue to illustrate age differences with regard to the *content* of the talk in the dialogue and the *language* used.

Aim:	- To listen to a song and write down vocabulary items from the song
	- To collaborate in pairs to write a dialogue
	- To perform the dialogue in front of the class
	- To discuss the nature of the relationship between the older and younger speakers as portrayed in the dialogues
Level:	Intermediate
Time:	60 minutes
Materials:	An audio device to play the song; student notebooks
Preparation:	- Have available the song to play.
	- Prepare guidelines for writing the poem.

Language practice	
Skills?	listening, writing, speaking
What?	listening to a song, writing and performing a dialogue, age-appropriate vocabulary, direct speech
How?	collaborating and performing in pairs, whole-class discussion

Procedure

1. Inform students they will be writing a dialogue together in pairs.
2. As a warm-up and to provide students with a working vocabulary play them a song about age (differences) and ask them to write down some of the keywords they hear. The song should preferably be one they are not familiar with and be above their listening proficiency level.

93

From Implications to Application

Students will have to listen carefully to the lyrics. You can check the appropriateness of lyrics by accessing numerous webpages on the internet (search 'song lyrics'). The Beatles' song 'When I'm sixty-four' is a good, safe example, but you can find others if you search 'songs about age differences'. Your choice will need to be sensitive to the age and cultural backgrounds of students in your class.

3. Give instructions for writing the dialogue collaboratively in pairs: (a) an older and a younger person having a conversation, (b) about 10 to 15 lines, (c) the *content* should exhibit the age difference, and (d) the *language* should reveal the age difference.

4. In pairs, students write the dialogue, giving them about 20 to 30 minutes. They should write a draft, revise and edit it, and then produce the final version.

5. Ask pairs to role play their dialogue for another pair of students. Repeat until each pair has performed the dialogue a number of times to different pairs. (If the class is small, pairs could each take a turn to role play the dialogue in front of the whole class.)

6. Ask for a few volunteer pairs to role play their dialogue in front of the whole class.

7. After each of these dialogues is performed discuss the age differences reflected in the content and language in the dialogue. What does the content and language say about the *relationship* between the speakers? Is there respect, submissiveness, power play, impoliteness, humor? How does the language signify the identities of the speakers?

8. Display the dialogues on a board in the classroom and invite students to walk around and read them.

Teacher Reflection

For each of the following statements, answer YES or No and give a reason for your answer:

1. When I started my first teaching job, I was concerned about my age.
   YES/NO: _____

From Implications to Application

2. The age gap between me and my students has never been an issue for me.
   YES/NO: _____
3. I feel awkward when my students comment about my age.
   YES/NO: _____
4. I am comfortable being my age working in this institution.
   YES/NO: _____
5. The language I use in the classroom usually reflects my age.
   YES/NO: _____

Activity 17: The Clothes We Wear

Introduction

In this activity, students write a poem collaboratively in groups. Drawing on vocabulary from a written paragraph, students write a poem about the clothes a particular person wears. After poems are read aloud to the class, a discussion follows about how clothes project aspects of our identity.

Aim:	- To read a short story and select vocabulary items
	- To collaborate in groups to write a poem
	- To read the poem aloud to the class
	- To discuss the relationship between the clothes we wear and our identities
Level:	Intermediate
Time:	60 minutes
Materials:	The short story paragraph provided, student notebooks
Preparation:	- Print one copy of the short story for each student.
	- Prepare guidelines for writing the poem.

95

From Implications to Application

Language practice	
Skills?	reading, writing, speaking, reading aloud
What?	describing, descriptive vocabulary, creative writing
How?	independent reading, collaborating in groups

Procedure

1. Inform students they will be writing a poem together in groups.
2. To provide students with working vocabulary give them a copy of the short story below and ask them to read it carefully by themselves.

   Instead of driving to work as usual, Jacinda decided to take the bus because it looked like it might rain. There were streaks of blue in the sky, but the clouds were dark, and swirls of wind were beginning to shake the leaves on the tree outside her bedroom window. She grabbed her hat and coat and headed to the bus stop. When it arrived she noticed it was full and hesitated before climbing on board. She had to stand the whole way to work and spent the time looking at the passengers. They too were dressed for winter. Knitted scarves. Puffer jackets of all colors. "Everyone seems to be wearing them these days," she thought. Lots of denim, skinny jeans. Boots. The trip was boring until the very last moment—she heard a loud scream as the bus was pulling up to her stop. She thought someone had fallen or perhaps had been mugged! But very soon everyone began to clap and laugh. A woman sitting at the back of the bus wearing a bright red beanie had just received a text message saying she had been offered a job she had applied for. It was a scream of joy and excitement. This put Jacinda in a good mood for the rest of the day. As she stepped off the bus, careful not to step into any puddles with her leather shoes, she decided she may take the bus more often.

3. Student circle five words in the paragraph. They will use some of these words to write their poem.
4. Give instructions for writing the poem collaboratively: (a) focus on an individual person; (b) write at least 8 to 10 lines; (c) use

From Implications to Application

any style—rhyming not necessary; (d) write about the clothes the person wears—such as when, where, with whom, what they do when wearing those clothes; and (e) use as many of the circled words as possible, at least 10 from the group. Provide any further guidelines for writing the poem that you think your students might need.

5. In groups, students write the poem; give them about 20 minutes. They should write a draft, revise and edit it, and then produce the final version.

6. Monitor the activity to ensure participation by all students.

7. Ask for a volunteer from each group to read out their poem to the whole class.

8. After each poem has been read have a brief open discussion about the kind of person depicted in the poem. What do we learn about who they are? How does what they wear project their identities?

9. If there is time, each student could draw the person in the poem their group has written.

10. Display the written poems (and the drawings) on a board in the classroom and invite students to walk around and read them silently.

Teacher Reflection

Consider these questions:

1. Think about the clothes you wear to work every day?
   a. What do your clothes say about you *as a teacher*?
   b. What do you think your students think about your choice of clothing?
   c. Imagine wearing a different style of clothes. What would it be? How would this change how you are perceived by your students and your teacher colleagues?

2. Does your school have a dress code?
   a. If so, are you and your colleagues happy to adhere to it? Why? Why not?
   b. If not, what determines what you wear to work?

From Implications to Application

Activity 18: Why Is Facebook So Popular?

Introduction

Social media sites such as Facebook enjoy huge popularity in the world. Billions of people use Facebook around the world. It is very likely that most, if not all of your students, use these sites. It is important that they think about why they are attracted to Facebook and that they consider how they project themselves on their own online postings. Research is undecided as to whether Facebook is good or bad for us, but it is true that interacting with others on social media sites impacts on our sense of identity. This activity requires students to complete a worksheet that asks them to rank reasons for the popularity of Facebook and then to compare and discuss their views.

Aim	- To consider and evaluate social media use
	- To list explanations according to which are most plausible
	- To reflect on how Facebook users project their identities online
	- To defend choice in small group, inter-group, and whole-class arrangements
Level:	Intermediate
Time:	60 minutes
Materials:	If you have a Facebook account, you might show the class your Facebook page if you are happy to do so. Worksheet of reasons for students.
Preparation:	- Prepare copies of the worksheet.
	- Ensure access to the internet to show Facebook pages.

From Implications to Application

Language practice	
Skills?	listening, speaking
What?	listening and participating to a mini-lecture, analyzing given data, weighing up respective merits, justifying and negotiating choices in groups
How?	whole-class discussion, within- and between-group information sharing and negotiation

Procedure

1. Talk to the class about their use of Facebook. You might want to use your own Facebook page as an example, or you could use the page of a public figure or a professional group you are a member of. To start the discussion consider:

   a. the reasons that your students use Facebook
   b. how often they visit the Facebook site
   c. the image they project of themselves on Facebook and why
   d. how that image compares to their 'real-world' image
   e. what they like most about Facebook
   f. what they dislike about it
   g. whether they think their Facebook visits have a good, bad, or neutral effect on them
   h. how their identity is displayed through the Facebook activity

2. Hand out the worksheet and ask students to get together in small groups.
3. The worksheet contains a list of reason that have been put forward to explain Facebook's popularity. Ask the groups to select the three explanations they think best explain this popularity. They will need to talk among themselves to come to a decision.

99

From Implications to Application

4. Then ask each group to join another group where they discuss their choices.

   a. How much agreement is there between the two groups?
   b. What are the reasons for the ranking?

5. The original groups break away to discuss the new input. Does it change their choices?
6. The class comes together to compare how each group chose their list and whether they decided to modify their choices.
7. Discuss reasons for the initial choices and later modification. Students can use the worksheet to write notes of their discussion and their decisions. Include in the discussion opportunities for students to reflect on how their identities are displayed and performed during the Facebook activity.
8. Record on the board the three reasons that received the most votes.

   a. Do any of these address identity issues?
   b. Does their perceived real identity hide behind an online identity they wish to project?

9. Finally, ask the class if they think there are *other* reasons that have not been raised. Do they think these reasons are more important than the ones on the worksheet?

Extension

More advanced students can be asked to come up with their own reason for Facebook's popularity or they can be given just a few examples. Groups can also be asked to discuss the drawbacks of social media sites, for example:

- people are inclined to overshare, revealing too much of their personal identities, and are later embarrassed by what they have disclosed
- potential employers might not like what they see on Facebook pages
- Facebook shares data with advertisers
- people might be worried that their personal data and identity will be leaked

100

From Implications to Application

Students could be asked to write a short guide on *The Dos and Don'ts of Facebook*.

Teacher Reflection

Many professional associations and interest groups have their own (often private) Facebook page. These present opportunities for members to share and discuss their ideas, information, and personal experiences regarding the particular area of interest. Here are two examples:

The IATEFL Research Special Interest Group, an international group: www.facebook.com/groups/iateflresig/
TESOLANZ based in New Zealand, a regional group: www.facebook.com/groups/TESOLANZTalk/

Reflect on participating in such professionally-oriented social media groups, including sharing information and commenting on other people's posts:

1. Is this participation something *you* (might) engage in?
2. What are the benefits of this engagement?
3. How much would you be prepared to reveal about your ideas on language teaching and learning and your teaching practice?
4. What would or do you fear about participation?

Materials

Worksheet

	Reasons	Rankings (Round 1)	Rankings (Round 2)
1.	Facebook is a useful source of information. Users can read news and posts about issues around the world.		

101

	Reasons	Rankings (Round 1)	Rankings (Round 2)
2.	Facebook is great for entertainment. You can play games and watch videos. You can make new friends. It doesn't matter what time you go on Facebook—there is always someone to speak to and something to do.		
3.	Facebook is user friendly—users can text, comment, and like posts of other people just by clicking the mouse or tapping a screen.		
4.	Facebook's website is well constructed and attractive.		
5.	It's easy to find people using Facebook. We can find people we have lost contact with quite easily.		
6.	Facebook allows us to share photos, videos, feelings, locations. It allows us to change our status without any difficulties.		
7.	Facebook is continually updated with new features making it even more user friendly.		
8.	Facebook is the best site of its kind. The competition doesn't come close.		
9.	Facebook bans nudity and pornography. Parents don't have to be concerned about what their children are seeing when they are on Facebook.		

From Implications to Application

Reasons	Rankings (Round 1)	Rankings (Round 2)
10. Facebook security is usually good.		
11. Facebook allows us to present ourselves as we want others to see us.		
12. When bad things happen to us, we can tell our friends on Facebook and they can show their sympathy by sending us a message.		

Activity 19: Idiomatic Language

Introduction

All languages have idiomatic expressions that are often colorful and humorous. Students are often introduced to English idiomatic expressions, but little recognition is given to the idioms used in their own languages. In this activity, students are given an opportunity to share these expressions with the class while engaging with idiomatic English.

Aim:
- To promote the understanding and use of idiomatic English
- To encourage appreciation of the idioms in students' first languages
- To understand the difference between the literal and figurative meaning of words

Level: Intermediate

Time: 50 minutes

Materials: A list of idioms in English but can also be in other languages. A worksheet is provided.

Preparation: Prepare copies of the worksheets provided for each student.

103

From Implications to Application

Language practice	
Skills?	listening, speaking, writing
What?	comparing English idioms with idioms from other languages noting similar and contradictory idioms, literal and figurative meanings
How?	whole-class discussion, group discussion, group presentation, completing worksheet in a group

Procedure

1. Talk to the students about idiomatic language. Explain that the meaning of an idiom cannot be worked out simply by knowing what the individual words in the idiom mean. Idioms have a *culturally* understood meaning. Use examples like the ones below. It can be very difficult to understand idioms for people when learning a language because the words don't mean what they should!

    Croatian idiom: *Pūst pìlìtes*
    Literally means, "to blow little ducks," but what it really means is to talk nonsense or to lie.
    Russian idiom: *Когда рак На горе CBùTHeT*
    Literally means, "when a lobster whistles on top of a mountain," but it really means it's never going to happen.

2. Ask students to get into groups that share a first language. If this is not possible, students can work individually.
3. Students are then asked to think of an idiom in their own language and translate the idiom literally into English.
4. They are then asked to draw a picture that illustrates the literal meaning (e.g., someone blowing ducks out of their mouth).
5. The group then discusses how they would explain the meaning of the idiom to an English speaking person.
6. The groups are then given the opportunity to present their idiom (and picture) to the rest of the class.

104

From Implications to Application

7. They will demonstrate how they would explain the meaning of the idiom to an English speaking person.
8. Ask students to get back into groups and complete the worksheet. They can help each other work out the meanings of the idioms or they can use online resources.
9. As a whole class, discuss whether the students' languages have idioms with similar meanings. Do the idioms reflect any cultural norms or ways of life (e.g., respect for age, the value of knowledge or hard work)?

Extension/Variation

More advanced students could be asked to find English idioms that have similar meanings. They could be asked to explain which of these idioms they prefer and why. Perhaps they like the mental picture conjured up by a particular idiom.

Elementary students could be given a list of idioms and pictures that illustrate these idioms. These illustrations are freely available on the internet. Students would then need to link the pictures and the idioms and try to work out the meaning.

Teacher Reflection

There's a well-known idiomatic expression related to teaching that goes as follows:

Those who can, do; those who can't, teach.

How does this idiom make you feel? How would you explain your response to someone who is not in the teaching profession?

Materials

Group Worksheet

Look at the idioms listed. Discuss what they mean in your group. Then find the idioms that contradict each other. List them in the table.

105

From Implications to Application

You're never too old to learn.
Birds of a feather flock together.
He who hesitates is lost.
Clothes make the man.
A penny saved is a penny earned.
Absence makes the heart grow fonder.
You can't teach an old dog new tricks.
Out of sight, out of mind.
Opposites attract.
Don't judge a book by its cover.
Look before you leap.
Penny wise, pound foolish.

Match the two idioms that appear to contradict each other.

Idiom	Contradicting idiom

Activity 20: Make Your Own Cartoon

Introduction

In this activity, students explore stereotypes about people. For example, Irish people are often depicted as not being very clever, and Scottish people are supposed to be very mean. These stereotypes are often used as jokes. Students will know jokes like this about their own and other cultures or nationalities. In the activity, students ascribe these stereotyped entities to characters in a story or a joke. They do this by drawing simple cartoons. This activity gives students the scope to write the dialogue for the characters in the cartoon. They are also required to use direct and indirect speech.

106

From Implications to Application

Aim:	- To understand and practice direct and indirect speech
	- To examine the changes that are made when direct speech is reported
	- To tell a joke or story in direct speech
	- To retell the joke or story in indirect speech
Level:	Intermediate
Time:	60 minutes
Materials:	Video clips showing students how to draw stick figures. There are numerous YouTube clips that illustrate how one can draw stick figures in action (search for "drawing stick figures").
	- A cartoon with stick figures telling a story or a joke, preferably in a series of pictures. You could find some on YouTube or you might want to draw your own short cartoon, perhaps showing you talking to your students.
	- Make a copy for each student or have it up on the board so that they can all see it.
	- Sheets with pictures of stick figures in various positions and performing different actions as samples that can be distributed to students.
	- Copies of a selection of jokes written in indirect speech or a number of stories that can be distributed to students (two examples are provided).
Preparation:	- Try drawing a number of stick figures yourself so that you can demonstrate to students how easy it is.
	- Prepare copies of the pictures of stick figures and copies of the jokes and short stories for each student.

107

From Implications to Application

Language practice	
Skills?	listening, speaking, writing, visual literary
What?	using direct speech to tell a story or joke, using indirect speech to tell a story or joke, writing dialogue in a cartoon, writing indirect speech
How?	working individually to draw cartoons using speech bubbles, using others' cartoons to practice writing indirect speech

Procedure

1. Tell the students that they will be drawing their own cartoons. Explain to them that the video will help them to draw simple stick figures.
2. Play the video and give the students copies of the sample sheet of stick figures in various positions.
3. Give the students the cartoon with stick figures. Ask them about the characters in the cartoon or get them to discuss these characters with each other.

   a. What do they think about the characters?
   b. Are they nice people?
   c. Would the students like them as friends?
   d. What do think about their personality or identity?

4. Then ask the students to look at the way in which the story is told. This is done mainly through direct speech in a speech bubble or reveals the characters' thoughts in a thought bubble. If extra information is included, this is usually given very briefly in just a few words.
5. Examine the language in the cartoon and ask student to report what was said. Write their answer on the board and then ask them to identify what changes have been made in the reported speech.

From Implications to Application

6. Next ask students to draw their own cartoons. Encourage them to use their own jokes and stories about stereotypes but you can also distribute the copies of the jokes and stories you have prepared. They can be as simple as these two:

   a. Two Irishmen were working very hard in a park in Dublin. The one in front would dig a hole, and then his partner would fill the hole in. They worked across a very large area in the park watched by a number of puzzled people. Eventually, one of the people watching went up to the men and told them how impressed he was by how hard they were working. However, he was puzzled by what they were doing. He could not understand why they were digging a hole only to fill it up. The two men stopped to take a rest, and one of them explained that they were actually part of a three-man team. The second person in the team was the one who planted the trees, but he was sick, so they were having to do the job without him.

   b. Jock the Scotsman was on his way to the local bar. He turned to his wife and told her to put on her coat and scarf. She was really pleased because she thought he was asking her to go to the bar with him. He told her that he wasn't inviting her out. He simply wanted to turn off the central heating to save money while he was in the bar.

7. Before students begin constructing their cartoons, have a brief discussion about the risks of portraying stereotypes:

   a. Do the cartoons reinforce stereotypes?
   b. Ask students how they would feel about others making fun of their culture or nation.
   c. Where does humor end and insult begin?
   d. What does 'hate speech' mean, and what are its consequences for society?

   These are big questions, but it would be a good idea to touch on them briefly before the activity gets going. They could be

From Implications to Application

followed up in a later lesson, particularly with more advanced classes.

8. After the students have completed their cartoons, ask them to get into pairs.

   a. They then swap their cartoons with another student.
   b. Students may need to explain their cartoons to each other if the meaning is not immediately evident to the reader.
   c. Ask students to discuss how the identities of the characters in the cartoon are depicted.

9. If there is time and space, ask some students to draw their cartoons on the board for all to see (or they could walk around and share them face to face.)
10. The students then rewrite their joke or story in indirect speech (this could be done in a follow-up lesson).

Extension

More advanced students could use complex storylines or literary works which they translate into cartoons. They could be asked to explain why they have depicted a character in a certain way. There are numerous examples on the internet of Shakespearean plays in comic form. If students are studying a prescribed literary work, this would be an excellent way for them to incorporate language learning into their literature classes. Finally, students could be encouraged to write their own storylines and develop original cartoons.

Teacher Reflection

Quite often humor deals in stereotypes. This is clearly illustrated in number 6 in the Procedures. Teachers, of course, are also stereotyped. If anyone thinks back to the teachers they had during their school days, they would remember many funny stories about them. And these stories (the characteristics associated with the

From Implications to Application

> teachers) would be common to many other teachers as well. Think back to your own teachers:
>
> 1. Who was the funniest? Why?
> 2. Who was the most serious, someone you might have disliked or feared?
> 3. Which teacher do you think your classmates would all remember and tell stories about?
> 4. How do you think *you* would be stereotyped by your students in future years?

Activity 21: There's a Little Bit of Good in Everyone

Introduction

In this activity, students will discuss personality traits and consider the drawbacks of 'good' traits and the possible advantages of 'bad' ones. Individually, students will think about their own personalities and complete a table showing how these traits affect their lives and those around them.

Aim:	- To understand and define 'good' and 'bad' personality traits - To challenge accepted stereotypes - To consider the consequences of projecting personality traits
Level:	Intermediate
Time:	60 minutes
Materials:	A group worksheet and an individual worksheet are provided
Preparation:	Prepare copies of the worksheets provided for each student.

111

From Implications to Application

Language practice	
Skills?	listening, speaking
What?	discussing personality traits, defining 'good' and 'bad' traits, challenging accepted ideas of what is positive and negative
How?	whole-class discussion, completing worksheet in groups, individually completing worksheets

Procedure

1. Have a discussion with the class along the following lines. We all have personality traits that are regarded as good (e.g., loyalty and kindness) and those that are regarded as bad (e.g., selfishness and laziness). However, there are downsides to good traits and advantages to bad traits. You might be someone who prides yourself on your loyalty, that you always stand by your friends. What will you do in a situation when your friend is behaving badly or doing something that you know is wrong? Will you still remain loyal to that person? Should you?

    Bad personality traits can also have advantages. Lazy people don't like having to work hard, so they try to find ways to do things more quickly or easily. This can lead to better and more efficient ways of working. Bill Gates said, "I choose a lazy person to do a hard job because a lazy person will find an easy way to do it."
2. Ask students to get into groups and consider the group worksheet that has a table with 'good' and 'bad' traits. Students need to think about what is good and bad about the good trait and what is bad and good about the bad trait.
3. If space allows, students can move around the room comparing their ideas with other groups, giving reasons for their choices.
4. After the group discussion, ask students to work on the individual worksheet.
5. If there is sufficient time, you might like to bring the class back together for a final discussion around the complex nature of good and bad personality traits.

From Implications to Application

Extension

With advanced students, you might like to consider job interviews in which candidates are often asked what their strengths and weaknesses are. There is a lot of advice on what candidates should present as their weaknesses (e.g., I work too hard; I'm a perfectionist). Of course, these are not really meant to be seen as weaknesses but as strengths! Students could work on presenting accepted 'bad' traits (e.g., laziness) in a better light, or they could take on the role of the interviewer and ask probing questions. Role play in pairs would work well for this interview activity.

Teacher Reflection

Consider these questions:

1. What is the difference between *personality* and *identity*? How are they related?
2. How do *your* personality traits affect your teacher identity?
3. How do they affect your teaching *practice*?
4. What personality do you project to your students? How will they remember you in years to come?

Materials

Group Worksheets

Complete this worksheet in your group:

Good and bad traits	What is positive about this trait?	What is negative about this trait?
Kind		
Impatient		
Supportive		
Selfish		
Confident		
Indecisive		

From Implications to Application

Individual Worksheets

Select one good trait and one bad trait that make up part of *your* personality and then complete the table below:

Good Trait	How does this help you?	How does this hinder you?	How could you use this knowledge of yourself more wisely?
Bad Trait	How does this help you?	How does this hinder you?	How could you use this knowledge of yourself more wisely?

Activity 22: Proverbs and You

Introduction

Proverbs are traditional sayings that capture a truth based on common sense or experience. All languages have their own unique proverbs that are part of speakers' everyday language. In this activity, students will talk about proverbs in their own languages and work out the meaning of well-known English sayings. They will then choose one of the proverbs they have just learned and illustrate its meaning with an incident from their own lives.

Aim:	- To understanding English proverbs
	- To link proverbs to their meanings

114

From Implications to Application

- To illustrate the meaning of a proverb by referring to something that has happened in one's life
- to write a paragraph about a life experience

Level: Intermediate

Time: 60 minutes

Materials: Individual and pair-work worksheets are provided.

Preparation: - Think about proverbs that you are familiar with. They do not have to be English proverbs. Think about how you would explain the meanings of these proverbs to your students.
- Prepare copies of the worksheets provided for each student.

Language practice	
Skills?	writing, critical thinking
What?	discussing proverbs and their meanings, linking proverbs to what happens in everyday life, writing a paragraph about this everyday incident
How?	completing a worksheet in pairs, individually writing a paragraph

Procedure

1. Talk to the class about proverbs. Give the students the examples you have prepared. Then ask them to give examples of proverbs from their own languages and explain the meanings to the rest of the class. It might be interesting to compare different proverbs that have the same or similar meaning. You could discuss:

   a. What do the proverbs say about a particular culture?
   b. Do proverbs give advice about how to live our lives? Why?
   c. Who actually uses proverbs?
   d. Do proverbs reflect who we are and how we conduct our lives in society?

115

From Implications to Application

2. Ask students to form pairs. Give each student a copy of the worksheet provided.
3. Ask the pairs to match each proverb with its meaning (Part A). Pairs might need to consult each other.
4. When the pairs have finished, discuss the proverbs and their meanings. Go back to questions a to d above.
5. Then ask the students to complete the worksheet individually (Part B).
6. The paragraph writing could be completed for homework. If they make good stories, students could read them out to the whole class or within groups.

Extension

Students could find English proverbs that originate in the Bible or other religious texts or famous sayings (often referred to as 'golden proverbs') from Shakespeare's works. An internet search would be easy to do. They could be asked to explain the meanings of these expressions. They could then look for expression with similar meanings in their own languages and compare them with the English proverbs. What are the similarities? What are the differences?

Teacher Reflection

Consider these proverbs related to teaching. Think of them in relation to yourself and the work you do. What is your response to each one?

1. A wise teacher makes learning a joy.
2. If the pupil is smart, the teacher gets the credit.
3. Teach thy tongue to say, "I do not know."
4. Give a man a fish, and you feed him for a day. Teach a man to fish, and you feed him for a lifetime.
5. The mistakes of others are good teachers.
6. He who does not research has nothing to teach.

From Implications to Application

7. Experience is the best teacher.

8. The world teaches you more than your supervisor.

[Source: https://proverbicals.com/teaching-proverbs]

Materials

Part A: Group Work

Match the proverb with its meaning. Draw a line connecting the proverb and its correct meaning.

Proverb		Meaning
The grass is greener on the other side of the fence.		If you have admirable goals but never follow through with action, there may be unfortunate consequences.
A bird in hand is worth two in the bush.		Don't interfere in a situation that is presently causing no problems but may well do so as a result of such interference.
The road to hell is paved with good intentions.		You use this proverb to say that the things other people have or their situations always look better than your own even when they are not really so.
The squeaky wheel gets the grease.		When the need for something becomes essential, you are forced to find ways of getting or achieving it.
Those who live in glass houses shouldn't throw stones.		If you are someone who is vulnerable to criticism about a certain issue, you should not criticize others about the same issue.

(Continued)

117

From Implications to Application

Proverb		Meaning
Necessity is the mother of invention.		People who complain the most are the ones who get attention or what they want.
Let sleeping dogs lie.		Possessing something is better than taking the chance of losing it to attain something else that seems more desirable.

Part B: Individual Work

Select one of the proverbs from the list. Think about something that happened in your own life that illustrates the meaning of the proverb. Then write a paragraph about this experience. An example is provided.

When I was in primary school, I really liked my science teacher. She made the lessons interesting, and I enjoyed all her classes. I wanted to impress her, so I thought my opportunity had come when she set us all individual projects. We had to choose something that we had studied in class and read up around the topic. Our teacher said that we should aim to write something that would make people as interested in the topic as we were. She said we could do this any way we liked, and she encouraged us to use our initiative. I spent a long time thinking about the topic, and finally I decided that the best way to interest other kids was to link it to subjects that I knew they enjoyed.
I decided that I was going to talk about volcanoes and volcanic eruptions. I thought it would be really nice if I used superheroes when I was talking about eruptions. I made up a little story about eruptions. I wanted to talk about how powerful these eruptions can be when they throw rocks and boulders into the air, so I used the idea of Superman. I said that it was as if Superman was standing inside the mountain hurling rocks and boulders at alien spaceships in the sky. I drew pictures of Superman

From Implications to Application

throwing the rocks, and I even had different spaceships. I spent a lot of time working on the project, and I was very proud of it. I was sure I would get a really good mark. I couldn't wait to get it back! Unfortunately, when it was returned, I was very disappointed. The teacher said that she thought it was a bit childish using Superman in the science project, and she didn't like my drawings. I got a really low grade. I guess *I shouldn't have counted my chickens before they were hatched*.

Activity 23: Justifying Your Opinion

Introduction

In an earlier activity (*Activity 11: Chickens in Cages*), students were asked to identify the pros and cons of caged poultry farming. Students' decisions about what they do and do not eat might simply be a matter of what they enjoy, but increasingly, people are becoming more aware of environmental and ethical concerns about how the food they eat is produced. In this activity, they will be asked which side they agree with and why. They will be asked to justify their choice using language that is easily understood. The point is that in expressing an opinion, one is expressing (and therefore projecting) an identity.

This activity does not need to follow *Activity 11*. If you prefer, you can ask students to come up with the pros and cons of issues such as euthanasia or same-sex marriage. You will need to provide students with texts on the issue you have chosen, one in formal language and the other in less formal language. You will be able to source these easily on the internet.

Aim:
- To justify an opinion
- To identify differences between formal and informal writing (vocabulary and syntax)
- To summarize arguments succinctly

119

From Implications to Application

- To rewrite formal arguments informally
- To write persuasively using available evidence

Level: Advanced
Time: 60 minutes
Material: Students can use the worksheets completed in *Activity 11*.
Preparation: If needed, ensure that students have the necessary worksheets to consult.

Language practice	
Skills?	reading, writing
What?	discussing pros and cons of a controversial issue, writing an opinion piece, distinguishing formal and informal writing
How?	reviewing information as a group, writing individually

Procedure   (using worksheets from *Activity 11: Chickens in Cages*)

1. Ask students to use the worksheets they completed earlier.
2. Tell them that they will now be asked which side of the argument they agree with.

   a. Those who believe farmers should be allowed to keep chickens in cages.
   b. Those who believe farmers should not be allowed to keep chickens in cages.

3. Students will then be required to write a short opinion piece (400–500 words) for a local newspaper explaining why they believe cage farming of chickens should or should not be allowed.
4. They will use the worksheets they completed to justify their point of view. They will also be required to argue *against* the other perspective in a balanced and reasoned way.
5. Their attention will be drawn to the kind of language used in the original worksheet. The language for their opinion piece should be personal and informal.

120

From Implications to Application

Procedure   (NOT using worksheets from *Activity 11: Chickens in Cages*)

1. Give students the texts you have sourced.
2. Tell them that they will need to decide which side of the argument they support.
3. Students will then be required to write a short opinion piece (400–500 words) for a local newspaper explaining why they believe that [your topic] should/should not be allowed.
4. They will also be required to argue *against* the other perspective in a balanced and reasoned way.
5. Their attention should be drawn to the kind of language used in the texts you have given them. The language for the opinion piece should be personal and informal.

Variation

There are numerous other topics that could also be used for opinion pieces (e.g., immigration policies, the use of English as medium of instruction in higher education, the use of animals in medical experiments). Students could also be given informal pieces of writing from magazines or newspapers and they could be asked to rewrite them more formally.

Teacher Reflection

Students do not always feel comfortable expressing their opinions about certain issues in the classroom because it will reveal too much about what kind of person they are. The issues can be controversial and the opinions contested, which could cause students to feel threatened.

1. Do you strive to create a safe space for your students to express their opinions? How do you achieve this?
2. Are they able to be who they want to be?
3. What boundaries should you set? Are there topics or issues that you do not allow to be discussed in your classroom?
4. Do *you* feel free to express your own opinions about controversial matters? What limits do you set yourself?

From Implications to Application

Activity 24: Pictures at an Exhibition

Introduction

It is common to find exhibitions in museums or art galleries about the history of an immigrant group or refugee settlement. Auckland Museum in New Zealand held an exhibition named *Being Chinese in Aoteoroa: A Photographic Journey* (Aoteoroa is the Māori name for New Zealand). The exhibition tells the story of Chinese settlers to New Zealand from the first Chinese settler through two centuries of settlement, including themes such as making a home in New Zealand and relationships with local people. In this activity, students research experiences of settlement in a new country and the cultural identities forged in this process. They work on curating an exhibition.

Aim:	- To develop a project that involves independent and group research
	- To collect sources of information from outside the classroom
	- To search the internet
	- To present a curated exhibition
Level:	Advanced
Time:	Students work on the project during class time, especially in the planning and preparation stages. But some work may be required outside of class time.
Materials:	Internet access to research and to locate pictures and photographs of people
Preparation:	Find online links to exhibitions about migrant groups or immigration or refugee resettlement. Possible sources are museum and art gallery web pages, such as:
	- Auckland Museum Presents New Exhibition, 'Being Chinese in Aotearoa: A Photographic Journey': www.aucklandmuseum.com/media/

122

From Implications to Application

media-releases/2016/being-chinese-in-aotearoa-
a-photographic-journey
- Immigration Museum, Melbourne, Australia:
https://museumsvictoria.com.au/immigration
museum/
- The Migration Museum in London: www.migration
museum.org/

Language practice	
Skills?	integrated skills
What?	(re)searching for information, writing notes, multimodal curating
How?	researching in groups, presenting in groups

Procedure

1. Focus students on the topic and direct them to any web-based description of an exhibition on the topic.
2. Tell students that this is a project they can work on in pairs or small groups. Their task is to work as curators to plan an exhibition to celebrate the immigration and settlement of a cultural group of interest to them. They will present a small-scale exhibition for the class (or school).
3. Students as 'curators' decide on the immigrant or refugee group and time period of focus. The scope can be limited to personal or family experiences or relate to a wider group.
4. Students suggest a *title* for their exhibition and devise a short oral introduction to it. They determine two or more themes (e.g., early days, starting work, education) and source pictures or photographs, such as family photos of children starting school or arriving in the country.
5. Students stage the exhibition physically in the classroom. They can select music or other sound media to play in the background of the exhibit.

123

From Implications to Application

6. The exhibition could also be presented online, in a closed Facebook group, for example, or a learning platform. This will require a written introduction and notes connecting the images.
7. Non-presenting students ask the curators about their exhibits. Questions could include why the themes were selected, what ideas about identity the exhibition tries to express, and their personal or family experiences of coming to a new country if they are immigrants.

Extension

Students could source additional information and prepare short written texts. They might talk to family members about their recollections of settlement and feelings of identity. In the process, students can make notes (or an audio recording) to add to the exhibit.

For elementary students, the project can be very largely visual. In this case, students collect and display pictures that represent immigrant or refugee experiences and identity in the new country.

Teacher Reflection

Answer YES or NO to the first question. Then consider the following statements and note your personal reaction. How does your reaction relate to (1) your relationships with your students, (2) your relationships with your teacher colleagues, and (3) your classroom practice?

Am I an immigrant? YES or NO

A. Immigration and race are very much interconnected.
B. Immigrants' religious practices can be problematic in some host communities in my town or city.
C. Immigrants bring opportunities for learning about new cultural experiences to all in our school.
D. Private schools for immigrants to practice their religions and cultures are acceptable.
E. *All* immigrants should learn the dominant language of the host country.

From Implications to Application

D. Recognizing Identities

Table 2.4 Recognizing identities: Activity titles and aims

Activity	Title	Aims
Activity 25	A Good Friend	• To identity characteristics of a friend • To use appropriate vocabulary to describe a good (and bad) friend • To share ideas about what a friend is • To construct four lists of descriptive words and phrases
Activity 26	Who Are These Women?	• To recognize identity features in pictures of two different women • To describe these features using appropriate vocabulary • To explain their choices to a partner and to compare choices • To write a short paragraph to explain the rationale for their choices
Activity 27	Film Critic	• To consider the various elements that make up a film • To take notes • To identify elements in the film and evaluate them • To use guidelines provided to review the film • To set aside personal preferences to evaluate how well the film is made

(*Continued*)

Table 2.4 (Continued)

Activity	Title	Aims
Activity 28	Identity Theft	• To create imaginary characters to use in a debate • To consider ways in which personal identity can be represented in words, numbers, and images (semiotics means) • To rank and debate the importance of these identity references • To discuss ways in which identity theft can be prevented
Activity 29	Teacher Roles	• To consider language teacher role and students' expectations of these • To write down their ideas and discuss these in groups and as a whole class • To reflect on personal experience as a language learner
Activity 30	Gendered Identities in Occupations	• To critically examine the characters portrayed in online language teaching materials • To reflect on how these may impose identities
Activity 31	Stereotyping	• To investigate stereotypes about students' own and other cultures • To report on stereotypes of one's own culture • To discuss these stereotypes in class • To explore advantages and disadvantages of stereotyping

Activity	Title	Aims
Activity 32	Questioning National Identities	• To identity characteristics of two or three countries' national identities • To transfer those national characteristics to people from those countries • To exchange ideas and information about national identity • To question the viability of the concept 'national identity'
Activity 33	Designing a Questionnaire	• To work out meanings of vocabulary items • To work in groups to design items for a questionnaire • To evaluate questionnaire items • To finalize a questionnaire on colors and personalities
Activity 34	Writing a Report	• To explain a research topic simply • To interpret data • To use tentative language • To write an introduction to report writing
Activity 35	No Laughing Matter	• To consider what we find amusing and how this differs from person to person • To find examples of English-language advertisements (ads) to illustrate humor that appeals to us • To consider whether humor is an effective marketing tool • To conduct a mini research project in class • To evaluate the findings of the project and write them up

(*Continued*)

From Implications to Application

Table 2.4 (Continued)

Activity	Title	Aims
Activity 36	The Language of Ads	• To examine the language used in ads • To examine the ways in which these words are presented • To discuss the effectiveness of the language • To examine the visual techniques used in highlighting certain words • To compare and contrast different views about the language of the ads

Activity 25: A Good Friend

Introduction

What are the characteristics of a good friend—and of someone who is not a good friend? This is the question considered in this activity. At an elementary level, the aim is for learners to generate vocabulary and short phrases that describe what a friend *is*, *is not*, *does*, and *says* and then to share their descriptions with each other drawing up four lists in the process.

Aim:	- To identity characteristics of a friend - To use appropriate vocabulary to describe a good (and bad) friend - To share ideas about what a friend is - To construct four lists of descriptive words and phrases
Level:	Elementary
Time:	60 minutes

128

From Implications to Application

Materials: A matrix diagram is provided.

Preparation: - Prepare one large matrix diagram (see below) for each student and draw the diagram on the board.
- Provide one or two sample words for each quadrant in the matrix.

Language practice	
Skills?	speaking, listening, vocabulary, critical thinking
What?	describing, predicting meaning, expressing an opinion
How?	silent reflection, independent work on a diagram, pair work, whole-class sharing

Procedure

1. Ask all students to reflect silently on what it means to be a friend. Ask them to think about what a 'good' friend is; they could think about their actual good friends. Ask them also to think about what a bad friend is (someone they do not want as a friend).
2. Hand out the matrix diagram with the four quadrants as drawn, one to each student. Explain what each quadrant means and provide them with a sample or two, for example:

   a. *Is*: honest, loyal
   b. *Does*: keep a secret, spend time with you
   c. *Says*: thank you, are you OK?
   d. *Is not*: nasty, fake

3. Ask students to fill their diagrams in independently, writing three or four items in each quadrant.
4. After a few minutes, when students have finished filling in their diagrams, ask them to get into pairs.

   a. One student reads out a word or phrase from their diagram, and the partner has to determine which quadrant the word or phrase comes from.

129

From Implications to Application

    b. This may require some negotiation, but when they get it right, the partner writes that word or phrase in their own diagram.

    c. The partner then takes a turn to read a word or phrase from their diagram, and so on.

    d. Continue until each student has a few new words or phrases (one or two per quadrant).

5. Next, ask students to move around the room and share some words or phrases from their lists with new partners, writing down new items in their diagrams as they proceed. By this stage, students should be generating a substantial list of words and phrases related to the characteristics of a good or bad friend.

6. When students are seated again, turn to your diagram on the board and ask for volunteers to call out items which you then write in the appropriate place on the board. Students should write any new items into their diagrams.

7. When doing this, take the opportunity to draw on the students' contributions to talk about what friendship means, how we identify friends, and how we identity as friends.

8. To end, have an open class discussion led by you. Focus on:

- Why is friendship important to us?
- How do friends change who we are and who we become?
- Who do we tend to exclude as friends? Why?

Extension

The three questions in the final point could serve as written composition (or paragraph) topics for more advanced learners.

Teacher Reflection

How important is friendship among teacher colleagues in a particular institution? Think about the place where you currently work, or where you have worked in the past.

130

> a. What are some of the benefits of having colleagues as friends?
> b. Do you have a close teacher friend? If so, what do you do together professionally?
> c. Do you collaborate in any classroom-based research activity? If not, could you?
> d. Do you agree with this statement? *You don't have to be friends with your colleagues; you just need to be able to work together.*

Materials

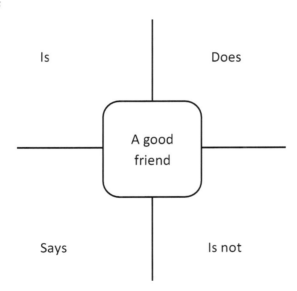

Activity 26: Who Are These Women?

Introduction

In this activity, pictures of two different looking women are provided on a worksheet together with 10 identity categories (e.g., age, ethnicity) and other characteristics that can be associated with the women. The simple activity involves assigning identity features to the two women and then comparing them with those assigned by other students.

From Implications to Application

Students then write a short paragraph to explain the rationale for their choices.

Aim:	- To recognize identity features in pictures of two different women
	- To describe these features using appropriate vocabulary
	- To explain their choices to a partner and to compare choices
	- To write a short paragraph to explain the rationale for their choices
Level:	Elementary
Time:	40 minutes
Materials:	A worksheet consisting of pictures of two different women is provided.
Preparation:	Prepare copies of the worksheet as presented for each student.

Language practice	
Skills?	vocabulary, speaking, writing
What?	using nouns and adjectives to describe identity, writing these onto a worksheet, comparing choices, writing a short paragraph
How?	completing the worksheet independently, discussing in pairs, writing a short paragraph independently

Procedure

1. Hand out the worksheet, one to each student.
2. Introduce the activity by explaining to the class how all people project their identities by the way they look including, for example, their facial features, their hair styles, the clothes they wear, and their actions. These identity features are then recognized by

132

From Implications to Application

others. Perhaps you could use a few pictures of people that you bring to class as examples.

3. Ask students to work independently filling in the worksheet by writing a noun or an adjective to describe the two women on the worksheet.

4. When they have finished, students work in pairs to explain their choices to the partners. Encourage the pairs to discuss their choices by comparing them and defending their own choices.

5. If space and time allow, students move around the room comparing their choices with other members of the class.

6. Asks students to work independently to write a short paragraph saying why they made the choices they did. The paragraph should address as many of the 10 identity characteristics on the worksheet as possible.

Extension

The activity could be repeated at a later stage in the course or repeated in the same class if time is available by providing a worksheet comparing pictures of two men or of a man and woman.

Teacher Reflection

Consider these questions:

1. How much notice do you take of the way you 'look' as a teacher?

2. Who do your students think you are? How do they recognize you as a professional? Does it matter to you?

3. Do you try to project yourself as a teacher differently outside of your school? Why or why not?

4. How do your recognize your future teacher self in, say, 10 years' time? What would your students think of you then?

133

From Implications to Application

Materials

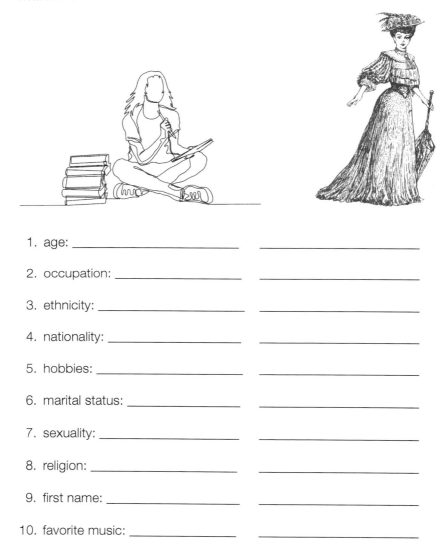

1. age: _____   _____

2. occupation: _____   _____

3. ethnicity: _____   _____

4. nationality: _____   _____

5. hobbies: _____   _____

6. marital status: _____   _____

7. sexuality: _____   _____

8. religion: _____   _____

9. first name: _____   _____

10. favorite music: _____   _____

Activity 27: Film Critic

Introduction

In this activity, students examine characters in a short film and decide what kind of people they are. They will also explore what they like and

From Implications to Application

don't like in films. What appeals and does not appeal to us is very much related to our backgrounds and past experiences—that is, who we are. Students are asked to recognize these likes and dislikes and then set them aside to judge whether they believe a film has met the criteria to be regarded as a good example of a genre.

Aim:	- To consider the various elements that make up a film
	- To take notes
	- To identify elements in the film and evaluate them
	- To use guidelines provided to review the film
	- To set aside personal preferences to evaluate how well the film is made
Level:	Intermediate
Time:	60 minutes
Materials:	A selection of short films without dialogue or with minimal dialogue ideally 5 to 15 minutes in length. *97%*, a Dutch short film (https://vimeo. com/143233550), is a good example. These short films are readily available on the internet. A work-sheet with relevant questions is provided.
Preparation:	Prepare copies of the worksheet as presented for each student.

Language practice	
Skills?	listening, speaking, writing
What?	watching a short film, evaluating it according to own likes and dislikes, evaluating it according to set criteria, writing a brief description and assessment in the form of a short report
How?	watching a short film in class, whole-class discussion, group work, writing in pairs

135

From Implications to Application

Procedure

1. Talk to the students about what they like in a film and then ask them what they think makes a good film. If time allows, you might want to view one short film with the class so that they can illustrate their discussion with examples.

2. Write the student ideas of what makes a good film up on the board. For films without dialogue, the following could serve as a guideline:

   a. interesting characters (the identities they portray and that we recognize because of the way the film is made)
   b. simple plot (story line)
   c. theme (message)
   d. believable ending

3. Hand out the worksheets and explain to the students that they will use these to take notes during and after the viewing.

4. Play the film asking students to write down keywords or short phrases to explain their views of the characters, plot, theme and ending.

5. After the viewing, give students a few minutes to complete their notes.

6. Students form groups of two or three students to discuss the worksheet using the keywords and phrases they identified during their viewing.

7. In pairs, students then finalize and write a simple review using the notes they made during the film and the later discussion.

8. Still in pairs, ask the students to continue their discussion, this time focusing particularly on the characters (or character) in the film, using these questions:

   a. Do you like the characters? Why or why not?
   b. What are their main defining features that stood out in the film?
   c. What do these features tell you about the identity of the character?
   d. Do you know people who are like the *main* character?
   e. How similar are *you* to the main character in the film?

From Implications to Application

Extension

This lesson lends itself very easily to extension work at all levels. For advanced students, short films with English dialogue can be used, and the components examined could be broadened to include conflict, resolution, structure, dialogue, visuals, and so on. These students might also want to write and film their own short story. Intermediate students could also be challenged by using films with more dialogue and by requiring lengthier written reviews.

Teacher Reflection

Imagine you are invited to write a film script for a short (10-minute) movie based on your school.

1. What action would you select to depict in the film? What would the film be about?
2. Who would be the main characters?
3. What would *your* role in the film be? How would you like the audience to see you?
4. What audience do you think would appreciate seeing the film?
5. How would they respond to the characters, including you, and the action?

Materials

Worksheet

1. Title of film: _____

2. Who are the characters? _____

3. Choose one character. What kind of person is he or she? _____

4. Where does the film take place? _____

5. What is the story about? _____

6. What is the message of the film? _____

137

From Implications to Application

7. Did you think the ending was good? _____

8. Did you like the film? Why? _____

9. Do you think other people would like the film? _____

10. What kind of people would like this film? Why? _____

Activity 28: Identity Theft

Introduction

There are many ways in which people's identities are projected
in concrete, semiotic terms, such as in their details presented on
passports, on social security cards, and membership cards to various
banks, social and recreational clubs, and employment institutions. We
are always at risk of these cards being lost or stolen or their contents
being accessed electronically through nefarious means such as
hacking. When this happens, the identity projected by these material
or online mediums is easily recognized and may be stolen or used for
illegal purposes. In this activity, learners debate which identity features
(numbers, words, images) are the most at risk of being recognized and
used for devious purposes and what we can do to avoid such theft.

Aim:	- To create imaginary characters to use in a debate
	- To consider ways in which personal identity can be represented in words, numbers, and images (semiotics means)
	- To rank and debate the importance of these identity references
	- To discuss ways in which identity theft can be prevented
Level:	Intermediate
Time:	60 minutes
Materials:	An outline of an identity card or document for each student (see Materials), or students can use their tablet or smart phone to create an identity document;

138

From Implications to Application

students' notebook for taking notes to describe their character and to prepare for the debate

Preparation: Prepare a blank identity card or document for each student on one sheet of paper.

Language practice	
Skills?	speaking, listening, writing
What?	debating, arguing, describing, note taking
How?	individual writing, note taking in pairs, debating in groups, whole-class discussion

Procedure

1. Begin by explaining to the class what *identity theft* means; that is, 'stealing' someone's identity (even a dead person's) and using it as one's own, usually for illegal purposes. For example, an identity could be used to secure a bank loan (which is then not paid back) or to obtain a passport.
2. Ask each student to work independently to create a character with its own identity by drawing and writing on the blank identity document you provide (or they can use a digital device). The document should have an *image* (a picture of a face), some *words* (name and other details, e.g., place of birth, or country of residence), and some *numbers* (identity number, date of birth).
3. In pairs, ask students to use their characters to imagine and discuss what could happen if someone stole the identity of their characters. In doing so, ask them to consider what would be worse to have stolen: the image on the identity document, the words, or the numbers.
4. Students write notes of their discussion in their notebooks.
5. Divide the class into three groups, or in a large class, multiple groupings of three groups.
6. In each grouping of three groups, one group will argue that *images* are worse to have stolen, one group will argue for *words*, and one group will argue for *numbers*.
7. Give them a short time to prepare a few points to support their argument.

139

From Implications to Application

8. To run the simple, informal debate, allow each group the chance to offer one point to support their argument and then allow the two other groups one rebuttal each. It might be a good idea to appoint a leader to manage the discussion.
9. Note: Like all debates, there are no right and wrong answers to this topic. The point is for students to discuss how identities can be recognized by others in concrete, semiotic terms and what the dangers are if those characteristics are 'stolen'. Furthermore, since the students will have created different characters (e.g., ages, nationalities, genders), their arguments will vary a lot.
10. After the discussion has continued for some time, ask students in all three groups to (try to) rank images, numbers, and words in terms of their risk to theft (i.e., most at risk to least at risk).
11. When they have done so, bring the class back together again.
12. Draw on the board three columns, headed: IMAGES, WORDS, NUMBERS.
13. Call on students to provide some of their points and write these down in the appropriate column. Ask them what their ranking was.
14. To end the activity, lead an open discussion about ways in which identity theft can be prevented, that is, how can we prevent people from accessing (recognizing) aspects of our identity and using them for illegal purposes?

Teacher Reflection

Working in a team in a school or other institution means that your colleagues often get to see what you do as a teacher: how you plan your lessons, the content of your classes, what you do in your classroom, what assessments you design and use, any professional reading you do, and any action research you might be involved in.

1. How do you feel about your colleagues using some of your ideas?
2. Do you willingly share innovations, successes, and failures with them?
3. Do they share innovations, successes, and failures with you?

From Implications to Application

> 4. Do you feel 'exposed' in some way as a teacher when others in your institution know and copy what you are doing? In what way, and why is this problematic for you?

Materials

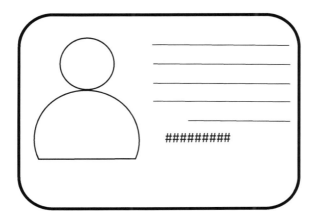

Activity 29: Teacher Roles

Introduction

What teachers do in the classrooms and the methodologies they use relate very much to their identities. Not all teachers teach the same, and there are different view and expectations regarding their practices. In this activity, students get the opportunity to consider different teacher roles, based on their experience as language learners, and to reflect on what their views and expectations of these roles are.

Aim:
- To consider language teacher roles and students' expectations of these
- To write down their ideas and discuss these in groups and as a whole class
- To reflect on personal experience as a language learner

141

From Implications to Application

Level:	Intermediate
Time:	50 minutes
Materials:	A worksheet for note making
Preparation:	- Reflect on the different roles language teachers have.
	- Become familiar with the four roles or identities listed on the worksheet in the Materials section.
	- Prepare copies of worksheets for students.

Language practice	
Skills?	listening, reading
What?	listening to explanation, discussing opinions in groups, writing brief note, meaning of *view* and *expect*
How?	whole-class instruction, working in groups and pairs, completing a worksheet independently

Procedure

1. Explain to students that language teachers want to help learners learn the language but have different ideas about how to do this and what their role is.
2. Highlight the meaning of *view* and *expect* or *expectation* and *autonomous learning*. Use the following information.

View	Expect
Some teachers and students *view* the teacher's role as transferring information from themselves to their students.	Some teachers *expect* students to do a lot of autonomous learning in the classroom.
Some teachers do not have this view. Some students do not have this view.	Some teachers do not expect this. Some students do not expect to do this.

142

From Implications to Application

3. Invite students to work in groups of three or four to discuss whether they share the view and expectation. Students make brief notes of their discussion to help with the report back.

4. Ask one student from each group to report on the ideas discussed while referring to the group's written notes.

5. Tell students that language teachers can have different roles and use different methods for teaching. Introduce the term *teaching methodology*.

6. Ask students to reflect, in their same groups, on the kind(s) of language teaching methodologies *they have experienced* and what the teacher and students generally did in the classroom. On a sheet of paper, ask students to draw two columns—one headed, *What the teacher did*, and the other, *What the learners did*. They then write down their observations in the appropriate column.

7. Ask groups to give one or two examples from their list and to comment on their and the teachers' views and expectations concerning the methodologies.

8. Explain the four types of teacher roles on the worksheet in the Materials, commenting on how they might relate to the methodologies teachers use in their classrooms.

   - **Instructor**: Focus on delivering content to the students.
   - **Facilitator**: Focus on organizing opportunities for students to work together with the support of the teacher.
   - **Manager**: Focus on discipline and maintaining a structured, well-organized learning environment.
   - **Friend**: Focus on getting along with students and treating them as equals.

9. Introduce the worksheet to the students and ask them to complete it individually. When they have done so, they compare and contrast their responses with a partner in pairs, expressing their personal views of the different roles.

10. To end the activity, conduct a whole-class discussion, focusing on the three questions below and drawing on the information the students wrote on their worksheet. During the discussion, try to include the idea that what the teacher does in the classroom,

143

From Implications to Application

their practice, relates to their *identity* as a teacher—how they see themselves and how others see them.

- Should teachers do what students expect or what they think is best for learning?
- Do students sometimes force teachers to be who they don't really want to be?
- Do some students expect their teacher's role to be the same as their teachers in the past?

Extension

One or more of the three questions in the last point could be used as topics for a class debate or a writing activity (for more advanced learners, the writing could be in the form of an essay).

Teacher Reflection

1. Do you sometimes find yourself doing what students expect even if it does not reflect your views on your role as a language teacher? Do you think that students impose a language teacher role and thus identity on you?
2. Consider how you might develop this activity to explain your teaching methodology and why you may not always do what some students might expect. Could you use this lesson to try to change entrenched points of view?

Materials

Worksheet for Note Making

	The instructor identity	The facilitator identity	The manager identity	The friend identity
What the teacher mainly does				

144

From Implications to Application

	The instructor identity	The facilitator identity	The manager identity	The friend identity
What the students mainly do				

Activity 30: Gendered Identities in Occupations

Introduction

Gender, social class, level of education, and occupation intersect in the workplace. This activity requires students to survey pictures in a unit or lesson of online language teaching materials to explore this intersection. They work in groups to summarize what they find, report back to the whole class, and write a short report in note form on the findings of the survey.

Aim:	- To critically examine the characters portrayed in online language teaching materials
	- To reflect on how these may impose identities
Level:	Intermediate
Time:	60 minutes
Materials:	- Students will need access to the internet, using a smart phone or tablet, or their institution's computers.
	- Select two online language learning units or lesson plans that include a number of pictures of people in everyday settings, particularly themes that include careers or work. Two popular sites are the following:
	- www.eslcafe.com
	- www.teachingenglish.org.uk

145

From Implications to Application

> **Preparation**: Make observations of the work sectors, careers, social classes, and genders of characters in the pictures in the two selected units or lessons.

Language practice	
Skills?	speaking, listening, writing
What?	describing, comparing (more than, not as many as), summary writing
How?	whole-class instruction, group work, reporting back to whole class

Procedure

1. Focus students' attention on the title of one of the units. Ask students to look over the pictures in that unit.
2. On the board, write *male and female, occupations*.
3. Using one picture as an example, provide sample sentences, such as:

   - *The picture shows five people. The three men are doctors, and the two women are students.*
   - *The picture shows three people. One woman is working as a receptionist and another as an engineer. The man is a pilot.*

   Introduce terms: *working class, middle class, service staff, professionals, tradespeople*
4. Put students in two groups (or multiple groupings of two groups in a large class). Students in Group A survey pictures in the first unit, and students in Group B survey pictures in the second unit.
5. Groups complete the grid in the Materials section and prepare to make a summary of findings of the survey orally to the whole class.
6. A student from each group presents the summary of findings.

146

From Implications to Application

7. Provide a focus on language forms that were used or could have been used in the summaries, such as *are shown/depicted as, more professionals than/not as many tradespeople as professionals are shown/depicted*.

8. Lead discussion about the findings and encourage critique, if relevant. Ask questions such as:

   - What kind of careers and workplaces are portrayed?
   - Is the course unit or lesson highlighting a particular social class at the expense of others?
   - What genders are shown? Are equal numbers of males and females shown?
   - Are particular career or workplace identities shown for males and females?
   - Does the selection of pictures represent the career or class interests or realities of the students or their families?

9. Groups (A and B) prepare a written report in note form on the findings of the survey and include suggestions for changing the selection of pictures if relevant.

Teacher Reflection

Consider this statement:

There are more female than male language teachers.

1. Why do you think this is so?
2. Is this the case in your institution?
3. What is the social status of language teachers in the context (local, regional, national) where you work? Does being a male or a female make a difference?
4. Are you proud to call yourself a language teacher? Are your friends and family proud of you?
5. Do you consider yourself to be a professional?

From Implications to Application

Materials

Use the following grid for the analysis of the pictures in the unit selected.

	Female	Male
Occupation		
Job description		
Social class		
Level of education		

Activity 31: Stereotyping

Introduction

The word *stereotype* was borrowed from the vocabulary of printing. A stereotype is a metal plate that is used to print the same character (e.g., a letter or symbol) over and over again. The character does not change. The word comes from the Greek in which *stereos* means 'firm', and 'typos' means print. Cultural stereotyping is when someone has an opinion of another person based on who they are, where they're from, or the language they speak without getting to know the individual. Positive stereotypes say good things about people from one country (e.g., Chinese students work hard). Negative stereotypes say bad things (e.g., Australians drink too much). In this activity, students are asked to examine stereotypes, both those held about them and those that they hold about others. They examine cultural stereotypes and decide whether they agree or disagree with them.

Aim:
- To investigate stereotypes about students' own and other cultures
- To report on stereotypes of one's own culture
- To discuss these stereotypes in class
- To explore advantages and disadvantages of stereotyping

From Implications to Application

Level: Intermediate
Time: 60 minutes
Materials: A worksheet is provided.
Preparation: Prepare a copy of the worksheet for each student.

Language practice	
Skills?	speaking, vocabulary
What?	comparing and contrasting different cultural groups
How?	whole-class discussion, completing worksheets individually

Procedure

1. Explore the idea of stereotyping with the whole class.
2. Consider the following stereotypes about Japanese and Germans and ask students to decide which of the stereotypes are positive and which are negative. Write the words on the board. Give students the opportunity to look up the words they don't know.

   a. **Japanese**—polite, disciplined, organized, irritable, fearful, neurotic, extroverted, competent.
   b. **Germans**—organized, boring, no sense of humor, conscientious, beer-bellied, punctual, big eaters, blindly follow rules.

3. Then ask students to consider their own cultures (or countries).

   a. What do you think other people think about your culture?
   b. What do outsiders believe about people in your cultures?
   c. Are you seen as hardworking or lazy?
   d. Are you friendly or standoffish?
   e. Are you trustworthy or not?

4. Hand out the worksheets one to each student. Ask students to fill in Part A. There is a space for students to indicate if they agree with *outsiders'* opinions of their cultures. Do they believe these opinions describe their cultures accurately?

149

From Implications to Application

5. Then students are asked to consider what stereotypes *they* believe accurately reflect their cultures. Ask them to complete Part B.
6. When the students have completed the worksheets, pin up the worksheets on the wall and allow students an opportunity to walk around the class and read them. Ask them to make notes of questions they would like to ask fellow students about the lists.
7. Then facilitate a class discussion where students ask each other about the lists and why they have indicated certain positive or negative features.
8. Finally, ask students to consider what is good and bad about stereotyping.

Extension

Ask students to go online and find advertisements (ads) that focus on a national culture. There are many of these. Students then send the URL of the ad to the teacher. In class, the teacher plays the ad to the class, and the student explains the cultural background and what cultural attribute is being highlighted (e.g., respect for elders). If the class is too large, students can work in groups.

Teacher Reflection

Consider these questions:

1. Do you think you are influenced in any way by the culture or nationality of your students?
2. Do you expect your students to behave and interact with each other in particular ways?
3. Do you expect students from different cultural groups or nationalities to interact with you in different ways?
4. How does this influence your relationships with your students?
5. How does this affect your classroom teaching practice?

From Implications to Application

Material

Worksheet

Part A

Other people's opinion			
My culture	**Positive stereotypes**	**Negative stereotypes**	**Agree/disagree**

Part B

My opinion		
My culture	**Positive stereotypes**	**Negative stereotypes**

Activity 32: Questioning National Identities

Introduction

The concept of national identity can be problematic in that it often represents a collective identity and ignores the individual people who make up those nations. In this activity, students explore the internet (starting with Wikipedia, for example) to identify characteristics of people from various nations. They transfer their understandings onto outline figures of people, marking them in a way that represents their nationalities, and in pairs they then ask

151

From Implications to Application

questions to discover the nationality of each other's marked figures. The activity also questions the concept of 'national identity' itself.

Aim:	- To identity characteristics of two or three countries' national identities
	- To transfer those national characteristics to people from those countries
	- To exchange ideas and information about national identity
	- To question the viability of the concept 'national identity'
Level:	Intermediate
Time:	60 minutes or spread over two lessons
Materials:	- Students will need access to the internet. They could use their smart phones, tablets, or institutional computers.
	- Students' workbooks to write notes
	- Blank outline figures of people for coloring, drawing or writing on (see Materials)
Preparation:	Photocopy three or four outline figures of people for each student, which could be on one sheet of paper.

Language practice	
Skills?	reading, speaking, critical thinking
What?	asking and answering questions, using semiotic resources appropriately, informal note taking, wh- and yes/no question forms
How?	independent internet searching, working in pairs, asking and answering questions in pairs, whole-class discussion

Procedure

1. Start the class by providing brief information about nation and nationality. Simply:

From Implications to Application

- Nations are countries.
- People from those countries are nationals from that country or they hold that country's nationality.
- Different nations are perceived to have different traditions and characteristics as do the people from those countries (e.g., the languages they speak, the way they dress, their facial features, their race, the things they eat, their music, their religions, and other beliefs and political systems).

2. Ask students to research on the internet two or three countries (depending on level and time available) on different continents to determine what some of their people's characteristics are. They could do a Google search or go directly to Wikipedia, for example:

- https://en.wikipedia.org/wiki/Colombia
- https://en.wikipedia.org/wiki/Cameroon
- https://en.wikipedia.org/wiki/Canada

3. This will require some research from the students, and you may need to give them some guidance regarding what to look for. Use some keywords from 1 above.
4. Students will need to take notes of the information they gather from their research.
5. Give to the students the sheet of paper with three or four outline figures of people; see Materials below.
6. Ask students to work independently (they could also work in pairs to do this) to represent their understanding of the characteristics of the people from two or three countries, including their own (they won't need to do an internet search for their own country; they can use their own experience; and if working in pairs, they will need to each do their own figure).
7. Let the students be creative about how they construct the country's people on the figure, but if they do get stuck, you could suggest:

- using colors
- adding words or phrases written on the figures (or in speech bubbles, for example)

153

From Implications to Application

- adding to the figure by drawing, such as clothing, facial features, food items, actions, or other objects
- using symbols (like flags) or musical notes or words of songs

8. When the students have finished the task, they work with a partner (or another pair). One by one each student takes a turn to show one of the figures to the other student and asks them to guess the nationality of the person represented by the figure (i.e., what country they come from). They do this by paying attention to the characteristics shown on the figure and asking questions, including wh- and yes/no questions, such as: Why is the person holding a green flag? Is the country in South America? What is the person standing on? What does the word 'queen' mean? Are those hats worn by women or men? Is the country Colombia?
9. Give students enough time to each have a few turns asking and answering questions about their figures.
10. When they have finished, they could write the name of the country under each figure and then attach their sheet of paper to a wall. Students can then move around to examine the figures and perhaps ask further questions from the students who constructed them.
11. To end the activity, as a whole-class discussion you could draw students' attention to the following two points:

- The people in the figure could have been constructed by the students in many different ways. (What is seen is the representation only of the student who did the internet research and who constructed the outline figure.)
- Not all people in the country would look the same. In other words, national identity is a collective, but people within that country have their own identities, too.

Extension/Variation

The information gathered from the internet search and written down in informal notes could be used for a writing activity. The information and the figures could also be used for oral presentations. Cross-reference to *Activity 31: Stereotyping* might be useful, and perhaps these activities could follow in a sequence.

154

From Implications to Application

Teacher Reflection

This reflection might be useful before the activity, but it can also be done afterward. Think about the following questions:

a. What country or countries are you from?
b. Do you 'represent' your country when you teach? If so, how?
c. What do your students think about your country? Are they from the same country as you?
d. Is your nationality an important part of your professional identity?
e. Take a moment to represent yourself on one of the outline figures in the Materials.
f. Would you be prepared to show it to one of your teacher colleagues?

Materials

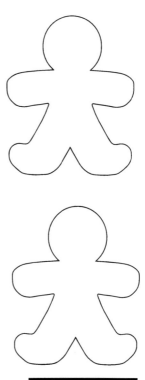

From Implications to Application

Activity 33: Designing a Questionnaire

Introduction

People are always interested in aspects of their own personalities. This activity uses this interest to ask students to consider whether certain colors are linked to personality traits. Students develop a simple questionnaire that can be administered to students in other classes.

Aim:	- To work out meanings of vocabulary items
	- To work in groups to design items for a questionnaire
	- To evaluate questionnaire items
	- To finalize a questionnaire on colors and personalities
Level:	Intermediate
Time:	60+ minutes
Materials:	Prepared cards, large sheets of paper, and markers
Preparation:	Prepare a set of cards colored blue, red, green, and yellow. The number of cards will depend on the size of the class. See Materials.

Language practice	
Skills?	speaking, writing, critical thinking
What?	designing statements to represent a concept, negotiating in groups, defending opinions
How?	class discussion, working in groups, collaborative writing

Procedure

1. Initiate a class discussion about colors. Perhaps students can name their favorite colors and say which colors they like to wear. Ask them whether they agree with psychologists who say that the colors we like tell a lot about us. Then tell them that they are going to develop a test that will allow people to see which color best represents them.

156

From Implications to Application

2. Explain that they are going to write statements with which people will either agree or disagree. But point out that we rarely completely disagree or completely agree with statements, and some claims we don't feel strongly about at all. So instead of asking people simply whether they agree or disagree with our statements, we are going to allow them to say how much they agree or disagree. Write the following on the board:

I think the colors people like tells us a lot about their personalities.

Strongly agree	Agree	Neither agree nor disagree	Disagree	Strongly disagree

What would they choose?

3. Now randomly distribute the prepared cards with the lists and ask students with the same color cards to form groups of three or four. The groups look at the word list and together work out what the words mean. They can use dictionaries (hard copies or online) if needed.

4. The group then turns the card over to read the statement that is devised to test for a personality trait associated with that color.

5. The group decides which of the personality traits (from the list of words) is being tested in that statement.

6. The groups then devise statements that test each of the other traits on their color cards following the example that has been supplied.

7. After the small groups have completed the statements, those groups with the same color come together and compare statements. These larger groups then choose what they believe are the five best statements to test for each personality trait associated with a particular color. (There will probably be a lot of duplication.)

8. Provide each group with a large piece of paper and a marker. The five chosen statements are written on the paper and put up on the wall. All the students then read and discuss the statements, commenting on:

   a. Whether they think it tests for the chosen trait
   b. Whether the statement is easy to understand

157

From Implications to Application

9. Work with the class to help them decide in which order the statements should be presented as a questionnaire to participants.

Variation

You could add more colors for the students to use (personality traits associated with various colors are available on the internet). The level of vocabulary on the lists could be varied according to the ability levels of the students. See the next activity, *Activity 34: Writing a Report*, which details how these questionnaires could be used to practice report writing.

Teacher Reflection

In classrooms we are surrounded by objects, including furniture, wall and floor coverings, and even stationery. Sometimes we have a choice about what these objects are and what color they are (e.g., the pens you use to mark or grade your students' work).

Take a look around your classroom and consider the colors you see. Do they reflect your personality in any way? Do the colors impact the way your students see you?

Take a look at the colors displayed in your school. What do they say about where you work? How do the colors make you feel?

Materials

Red

On one side of the red cards, write the following:

- competitive
- brave
- determined
- demanding
- independent

158

From Implications to Application

On the other side of the red cards, write:

Winning is very important to me.

Blue

On one side of the blue cards, write the following:

- cautious
- diligent
- precise
- objective
- disciplined

On the other side of the blue cards, write:

I like my work to be neat and accurate.

Green

On one side of the green cards, write the following:

- considerate
- supportive
- patient
- sharing
- conformist

On the other side of the green cards, write:

I don't mind waiting for other people.

Yellow

On one side of the yellow cards, write the following:

- sociable
- demonstrative
- enthusiastic
- optimistic
- outgoing

159

From Implications to Application

On the other side of the yellow cards, write:

I always think good things are going to happen.

Activity 34: Writing a Report

Introduction

This activity requires the cooperation of your fellow teachers. In the previous activity your students designed a questionnaire to see if colors were linked to certain personality traits. You will need to ask your fellow teachers if they would be willing to ask their students to complete the questionnaire developed in *Activity 33: Designing a Questionnaire*. After the analysis is completed, students will think about their own identities in relation to colors.

Aim:	- To explain a research topic simply
	- To interpret data
	- To use tentative language
	- To write an introduction to report writing
Level:	Intermediate
Time:	120 minutes or two 1-hour lessons
Materials:	Copies of completed questionnaires, example of returned questionnaire, and example of written report
Preparation:	- For this activity, you will need the help of your fellow teachers. Ask a few of them if they will allow their classes to complete the color questionnaire (*Activity 33: Designing a Questionnaire*).
	- These students will be asked to used code numbers or pseudonyms instead of their names. The questionnaires will be completed and handed back to the teacher.
	- Prepare copies of the example of the returned questionnaire (provided as example A in Materials).
	- Prepare copies of the example of the report model (provided as example B in Materials).
	- Prepare guidelines for writing the report.

160

From Implications to Application

- Prepare explanation of tentative language notes provided.
- Copy completed questionnaires to distribute to groups.

Language practice	
Skills?	speaking, writing, visual literacy
What?	using questionnaires to analyze data, writing reports, using tentative language
How?	whole-class discussions, analyzing data in groups, writing up reports collaboratively

Procedure

1. Introduce the activity by reminding students of the work they did designing the questionnaire in *Activity 33: Designing a Questionnaire*. Tell them that they are now going to analyze the data that was collected.
2. Ask students to form groups of three or four students. These do not have to be the same groups that worked to develop the questions used in the questionnaire.
3. Then randomly divide up the completed questionnaires among the groups, a few to each group.
4. Hand out a copy of the example of the returned questionnaire (example A) to each student.
5. Discuss with the students how the information has been represented in the graph.
6. The groups will then follow this method to develop a graph for each questionnaire they were given.
7. When the graphs have been completed, ask each group to draw one graph on the board, and get the students together for a class discussion.
8. With reference to their graphs, students will see that answers are quite varied (i.e., they might believe that competitive people will not be patient and supportive yet find that this is not always the case). Discuss with the class what this means (i.e., we need to be careful

From Implications to Application

about what conclusions we draw from the data). In reporting on the data, they should consider carefully:

a. Using tentative language:

- modals such as *might*, *may*, *can*, *could*, or *should*
- words such as *possibly*, *probably*, *unlikely*, or *certain*
- phrases such as *it is possible*, *it is probably*, or *it is unlikely*

b. Weighing up information:

- Are the answers high in one category?
- Are all the answers in this category high?
- What do you think we can say about the answers?
- What can we say if the answers are spread over all the categories?

c. Report vocabulary:

- biased or balanced

9. Hand out the example of a report (B in the Materials) to each student. Students return to their groups and discuss their graphs in light of the class discussion.
10. Then each group will collaborate to write up brief reports on each questionnaire using B as a model.
11. After the reports are finished, ask students how they would have answered the questionnaire. Give them an opportunity to complete their own graphs.
12. In groups they could consider whether they thought these graphs were a good depiction of their personalities.

a. Did their work on the questionnaire influence their answers?
b. Has their analysis of the results influenced the way they think of their own identities in relation to colors?

Teacher Reflection

1. You wake up in the morning and you think of the school day ahead—what color do you feel?

162

From Implications to Application

> 2. You go to bed at night and reflect on the school day just accomplished—what color do you feel?
> 3. You think of a teacher research project you are working on—what color do you feel?
> 4. Today a really shy student told your class she is lesbian—what color do you feel?
> 5. You're thinking of doing a new professional development course—what color do you feel?
> 6. You're being considered for promotion—what color do you feel?
> 7. Your favorite colleague will be co-teaching with you next semester—what color do you feel?
> 8. One of your students has missed the last three classes—what color do you feel?
> 9. A new student is the only refugee in your class—what color do you feel?
> 10. A student you don't like very much called you 'useless' in front of everyone—what color do you feel?

Materials

A. Example of Returned Questionnaire for JS (4 of the 20 questions)

Winning is very important to me.

Strongly agree	Agree	Neither agree nor disagree	Disagree	Strongly disagree

I like my work to be neat and accurate.

Strongly agree	Agree	Neither agree nor disagree	Disagree	Strongly disagree

From Implications to Application

I don't mind waiting for other people.

Strongly agree	Agree	Neither agree nor disagree	Disagree	Strongly disagree

I always think good things are going to happen.

Strongly agree	Agree	Neither agree nor disagree	Disagree	Strongly disagree

The students then assign a numerical value to each answer:

Strongly agree	=	5
Agree	=	4
Neither agree nor disagree	=	3
Disagree	=	2
Strongly disagree	=	1

JS's profile for four questions will look like this:

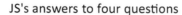

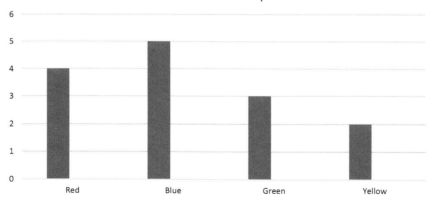

Once the students have charted all the answers they will see where JS's color preference lies.

From Implications to Application

B. *Example of Report*

Students should be given this example of a report to guide their first attempts.

Report for PW
Date . . .

Introduction

This report outlines the findings of a questionnaire completed by _____ and gives a brief indication of their significance.

Findings

In this questionnaire, PW had high scores in the red and yellow categories, the scores in the blue category were quite neutral, and the scores in the green category were low.

Conclusions

It appears that PW is probably quite competitive, determined, and independent. This is shown by the answers to (list the answers that support this). PW also appears to be social and enthusiastic and enjoys being with other people (list the answers that support this). However, PW might not always be very supportive or patient (list the answers that support this). Finally, PW does not seem to be particularly disciplined or hardworking (list the answers that support this).

Activity 35: No Laughing Matter

Introduction

What we find funny is very much a reflection of our identity. In this activity, students are asked to think about the type of humor that appeals to

165

From Implications to Application

them in advertisements and whether this would encourage them to buy a specific product. They are then asked to consider how other people experience humor, drawing on research done in the classroom.

Aim:	- To consider what we find amusing and how this differs from person to person
	- To find examples of English-language advertisements (ads) to illustrate humor that appeals to us
	- To consider whether humor is an effective marketing tool
	- To conduct a mini research project in class
	- To evaluate the findings of the project and write them up
Level:	Advanced
Time:	60 minutes
Materials:	Examples of ads that use humor (print/audio/video). Search YouTube for "funny ads" or "funny commercials."
Preparation:	- Students are asked to find three ads (print, audio, or video) that they find funny and will help sell a particular product.
	- Students to bring those to class.
	- Copy the short text in Procedure point 1 for each student.

Language practice	
Skills?	listening, reading, speaking, writing
What?	reading a short text, evaluating multimodal ads, assessing findings of a small group project, writing up the findings in the form of a short report
How?	listening as a whole class, discussion and evaluating in groups, writing a report independently

From Implications to Application

Procedure

1. Talk to students about the use of humor in advertising—the text below might be useful in guiding this discussion. Give students a copy of the text and summarize main points together with them.

   Making people laugh can be big business. Consumers are exposed to an enormous amount of advertising material that advertise many messages per day. Because they are exposed to so much advertising, they tend to be selective about what they pay attention to. If consumers aren't reading the ads put out by a particular company, this is going to have a detrimental effect on the company's bottom line—that is, how much money the company makes. One of the ways to make people pay attention is to get them to laugh. Research indicates that if a person thinks an ad is funny that person experiences positive emotions, which helps develop a positive attitude towards the product.
   So adding humor to an advertising campaign is a way for organizations to make an emotional connection with consumers. Of course, advertisers have to be very careful— what one person finds funny might not amuse another person at all. The worst case scenario is that it might offend them and then they will be disinclined to view the product favorably.

2. Divide students into groups of three to five (or whatever is appropriate for the size of your class) to begin a small project. Ask them to pool the ads they brought to class. They can view or listen to as many of these as possible on computers or phones.
3. Each member rates each ad out of ten according to two criteria:

   - how funny they think the add is (1 being not funny at all and 10 being extremely funny)
   - how effective the ad will be in helping to sell the product (1 being not effective at all and 10 being extremely effective)

167

From Implications to Application

4. The groups will then total the scores for each category and draw up two graphs showing how the ads were ranked for (a) humor and (b) effectiveness.
5. Using this information, students will write a report using the following headings (provide an appropriate word limit):

   a. Introduction: What the ads evaluation project was all about
   b. Process: How the ads were identified and scored
   c. Findings: Which ads were seen to be funniest /most effective. Here students will need to look at the scores. Was there one ad that was far more popular than the rest? Were a number of ads rated similarly?
   d. Discussion: Here the students will discuss why they thought the ads were ranked in this fashion. This is also an opportunity for students to say if they agree or disagree with the rankings and explain their reasoning.
   e. Conclusion: The student can make suggestions as to how ads can help market products.

6. After the students have produced their report, in pairs they can do a brief analysis of each other's reports, focusing on the following questions:

   a. Not everyone finds the same ad funny. What does that say about these people?
   b. Is a 'sense of humor' something we learn or something we are born with?
   c. How do we project our sense of humor to other people?
   d. How do we notice other people's sense of humor?

Extension/Variation

This lesson can be made accessible for other levels if more help is made available to the students. For example, you can select the ads yourself and give them to the students to discuss in groups or this can be done as a class exercise. Instead of writing up the results of the group work, students can present the main findings and conclusions in note form.

From Implications to Application

Teacher Reflection

Consider the extent to which you use humor in the classroom. Do you agree or disagree with the following statements?

1. Using humor in the classroom makes for more effective language learning.
2. I intentionally try to be funny in class.
3. I am a natural comic.
4. Students often laugh at my jokes.
5. Humor makes students feel more relaxed in class.
6. There is no place for student joking in my classroom.
7. My manager is a funny person.
8. My manager could do with a dose of humor.

Activity 36: The Language of Ads

Introduction

Advertisements (ads) are there to persuade us to buy certain products. Often they appeal to the identity we wish to project (e.g., a good sportsperson). In this activity, students are asked to think about what they find appealing and effective about the words employed in an ad and the way in which these words are presented.

Aim:
- To examine the language used in ads
- To examine the ways in which these words are presented
- To discuss the effectiveness of the language
- To examine the visual techniques used in highlighting certain words
- To compare and contrast different views about the language of the ads

Level: Advanced

169

From Implications to Application

Time: 60 minutes

Materials: Copies of ads *that include people* downloaded from the internet or taken from magazines or newspapers. Each ad must be examined by at least two groups.

Preparation: Prepare copies of the worksheet as presented for each group.

Language practice	
Skills?	speaking, writing
What?	analyzing the language of ads, identifying effective use of words, discussing the use of visual strategies in the presentation of language
How?	whole-class discussion, completing worksheets in groups

Procedure

1. Have a discussion with students about advertising. Explain that printed ads were originally meant to give information about products but that nowadays the focus is equally about capturing the reader's attention. Print texts have become shorter and advertisers employ novel words, phrases, and constructions. There is an emphasis on the creative use of language. The physical properties of the text (e.g., the font, size, and color) play an important part in drawing attention to the ad, as do the people in the ads — What do they look like? What are their identities? Would you want to be like them? Point out that ads can be aimed at a general audience or, as is often the case, a particular group, that is, the target audience.

2. Ask students to form groups of three or four students.

3. Give each group three different ads. Make sure that each ad will be discussed by at least two groups. Limiting the number of ads used will ensure that groups will be able to discuss their different views of the same ad.

From Implications to Application

4. Give each group a copy of the worksheet. Encourage students to explore the following in addition to working through the worksheet questions—you could write the following on the board:

a. Examine the *vocabulary* used in the ads, picking out the words that you think are important.
b. Identify *visual aids* that are used to highlight certain words (e.g., larger font, brighter colors, underlining).
c. Look for *phrases* that are used to attract the reader's attention.
d. Examine the *people* in the ads. What are they doing? What do they look like? How similar or different are they to you? Are they attractive, and what makes them so? Would you want to identify with them?

5. After the students have completed the worksheets, facilitate a class discussion about the ads, integrating language, visual aspects, and the identities of the characters in the ads and readers. Students will be able to consider why other groups found an ad more or less appealing or effective than they did.

Extension

Collect a number of pictures or photographs (not ads) with people in them. Place the students in groups and give each group a copy of the pictures or photographs. Ask them to design an ad using one of these pictures or photographs. Remind them of the work they did earlier when they were examining the language of ads. They can choose for themselves what product they wish to advertise and identify their own target audience. When they have finished, the groups can present their ads to the rest of the class, explaining who the target audience is and the decisions they made in choosing the language.

Teacher Reflection

We are all continually faced with persuasive language. Whether it is on the internet or in newspapers or magazines or on TV, we are bombarded with messages trying to persuade us to do

From Implications to Application

> something. The ways the messages are framed can often be very convincing and can play on our weaknesses and fears. We might find ourselves believing the promises they make even though we question whether such promises can actually be fulfilled.
>
> Does any of this apply to documents you come across in your professional life? Think carefully about the things you read, which you receive by post, by email, in your professional social media accounts. Do they force you to question what you do and what you think? Do they get you to change?

Materials

Group Worksheet

Questions to be completed for each ad

1. What product is advertised?

2. Who is the target audience?

    a. Why do you think so?

3. What words are highlighted?

    a. How is this done?

    b. Why do you think these words were chosen?

4. Which ad do you think has the most effective use of language?

    a. Why do you think so?

5. Who is in the ad?

    a. Are they appealing? Why or why not?

    b. How do they relate to who you are, as a reader of the ad?

6. Of the ads you examined which do you think is the most effective? Why do you think so?

From Implications to Application

E. Imagining Identities

Table 2.5 Imagining identities: Activity titles and aims

Activity	Title	Aims
Activity 37	What Kind of Wild Animal?	• To name various wild animals • To use adjectives to describe them • To give reasons for choice of best animal • To write a short paragraph
Activity 38	Me Flying High	• To create and describe images representing the language learning journey • To reflect on language learning identities and the language learning journey
Activity 39	My Dream Room	• To understand how our identities are reflected in choices that we make • To choose between various options in home decorating • To illustrate and explain these choices • To use conjunctions appropriately
Activity 40	Names for (Online) Gamers	• To consider online gamer identities • To justify the choice of gamer names • To relate gamer names to personal identity
Activity 41	The Aliens Have Landed	• To use descriptive adjectives • To give clear instructions • To listen carefully

(*Continued*)

173

Table 2.5 (Continued)

Activity	Title	Aims
Activity 42	Speaking English Tomorrow	• To imagine a future oriented speaking interaction • To anticipate language problems • To negotiate identity with an imagined interlocutor • To practice writing a coherent paragraph
Activity 43	Identity Quotes	• To introduce students to highly regarded identity quotes • To paraphrase these quotes • To discuss how they believe this quote could be presented in the form of a poster
Activity 44	Different Perspectives	• To identify ways to report an incident from different perspectives • To identify the kinds of words that represent these perspectives • To write a short newspaper article
Activity 45	What Makes Them Them?	• To use visual clues to construct an identity • To write a short description of a person depicted in a picture, commenting on their identity • To share and compare their description with other students

From Implications to Application

Activity	Title	Aims
Activity 46	Social Justice and Advertising	<ul><li>To examine the information and language in ads</li><li>To work in groups to discuss the choice of information</li><li>To examine the effectiveness of the language</li><li>To compare and contrast divergent views</li></ul>
Activity 47	Consumer Identity	<ul><li>To reflect on identity and consumerism</li><li>To categorize well-known English slogans using distinctions employed by the advertising industry</li><li>To identify the audience at which they are aimed</li><li>To evaluate how effective the slogans are</li></ul>
Activity 48	Transport of the Future	<ul><li>To discuss current forms of transport used by students</li><li>To identify the pros and cons of this transport</li><li>To read a passage on forms of transport in the future</li><li>To complete a worksheet on the advantages and disadvantages of new proposals</li></ul>

Activity 37: What Kind of Wild Animal?

Introduction

Animals have always played an important part in people's lives. Native Americans believe that different totem animals accompany you through

From Implications to Application

life, acting as guides and helping you achieve your goals. Even if we do not believe that an animal can be a spiritual guide, most of us have a favorite animal. In this activity, students are asked to think about wild animals and to choose which one they would like to be. Students watch a short video clip to help them choose an animal.

Aim:	- To name various wild animals
	- To use adjectives to describe them
	- To give reasons for choice of best animal
	- To write a short paragraph
Level:	Elementary
Time:	60 minutes
Materials:	A video clip of wild animals. YouTube offers a number of wildlife video clips (search 'wildlife video clips') to play to students. The video should prefer-ably be short, about two to three minutes long.
Preparation:	Have a list of all the animals shown in the clip in the order in which they appear.

Language practice	
Skills?	listening, speaking, writing, vocabulary
What?	listening to and watching a video clip, naming animals in the clip, explaining their choice of favorite animal, writing a short paragraph
How?	watching a video as a whole class, comparing lists in small groups, writing individually

Procedure

1. Tell the students that they will be identifying and talking about wild animals.
2. Give them an indication of how many animals they will see in the video clip you will be showing them and ask them to prepare a list of numbers so that they can fill in the names of the animals they see.

From Implications to Application

If they don't know the English names for the animals, they can write down the names in their own languages.

3. Play the video clip once, but before you do, let them know that you will be playing the clip again afterward and that you want them to write down the names of all the animals they recognize in the video clip.
4. Play the clip again. If necessary, pause it occasionally so that students have a chance to write down the names.
5. If necessary, play the clip for a last time, asking students to identify the animals.
6. Ask the class to get into small groups and to check each other's lists and fill any gaps.
7. Then go through the list of animals with the whole class.
8. Write the names on the board so the students can see all the animals' names, including those that they missed.
9. Ask the students which of the animals they like the most and why.
10. Write down the words that they use to describe the animals on the board. You might choose to add a few words that you would like them to add to their vocabulary. You could also introduce a few similes such as:

   a. as brave as a lion
   b. as wise as an owl
   c. as graceful as a swan

11. Then ask each student to choose one animal from the video that they would like to be.
12. Ask the students to write a short paragraph (just a few sentences) explaining why they have chosen that animal. In what way do they think this animal reflects who they are? They can use the vocabulary on the board to help them write the paragraphs.

Extension

This lesson can be approached in a different way for more advanced students. Video clips of different dog or cat breeds can be shown to the class. (Searching for videos introducing breeds of dogs or cats on YouTube will provide material.) These clips provide the names of the

177

From Implications to Application

different breeds and often list their characteristics as well. Students can be asked to write down the breeds that appeal to them giving the reasons for their selection. This description would cover the dogs' appearance as well as their characteristics.

Teacher Reflection

Reflect on your identity as a language teacher. When you conduct your professional life in your *classroom*, do any of the following animals make an appearance in your identity?

- tiger
- kitten
- snake
- butterfly

What about in your *institution* when you are outside of the classroom, away from your students?

Activity 38: Me Flying High

Introduction

In this activity, students create an image to represent their identities as language learners. They create a further image to represent their imagined future identities as language learners. The activity could be used at any stage on a language course.

Aim:	- To create and describe images representing the language learning journey
	- To reflect on language learning identities and the language learning journey
Level:	Elementary
Time:	50 minutes

178

From Implications to Application

Materials: Two images of kites: a box kite and a diamond kite

Preparation: Prepare the images of the two kites so that all students can see them, on a PowerPoint or large diagram, for example.

Language practice	
Skills?	listening, drawing, writing, speaking
What?	creating an image, adjectives of comparison, referring to future time, writing notes
How?	whole-class instruction, independent drawing and writing, online internet search, question and answer related to created image

Procedure

1. Let students know that the topic of the lesson is 'we are language learners'. The teacher introduces the two images of the kites (see Materials) and the terms *kite*, *box kite*, and *diamond kite*.

2. Elicit sentences from the students about the two kites, with prompts such as:

   - Can it fly?
   - Is it heavy?
   - Is it difficult to fly?
   - Is it easy to fly?
   - Does it take a long or a short time to make?

3. Take a few minutes to talk about your own learning of an additional language and compare your journey to the two kites, as follows:

   - The box kite is the early learning stage. At this stage, using the language is difficult. It takes a long time to learn the language. The box kite is difficult to make, and it takes a long time to get the kite off the ground.

179

From Implications to Application

- The second kite is the later stage. The kite flies easily. It is easy to make, and you can use the kite easily.

4. Ask students to create their own two images representing themselves as *present* and *future* language learners. They could draw their own images. Or you could refer them to online sites, such as Shutterstock, an online site of images in the public domain, where they could select images to represent themselves: www.shutterstock.com/

5. When students have finished creating their images, ask them to explain their images briefly in writing. Use prompts appropriate for elementary level, such as:

   a. It's a _____.

   b. See the _____.

   c. It can _____.

   d. But _____.

   e. I feel _____.

6. Display the images (and descriptions) for other students to see on the classroom wall. Students can walk around commenting on and asking questions about the images.

Extension

Later in the unit or in a more advanced class, the writing stage could be a fluency activity in which students write a lengthier description of the images and an explanation of their choice of images using less scaffolding.

Teacher Reflection

In this activity, you briefly described your own language learning journey to the students. In the space provided, draw an image of how you currently see yourself as a speaker of an additional language. Give your image a title.

From Implications to Application

Materials

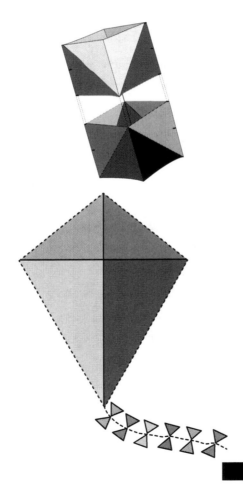

From Implications to Application

Activity 39: My Dream Room

Introduction

It is generally accepted that your home is a reflection of who you are. In other words, what you choose to surround yourself with tells us a great deal about your sense of identity. In this activity, students are asked to design their ideal bedroom, giving reasons for the choices they make. They explain their choices by completing sentences on a worksheet.

Aim:	- To understand how our identities are reflected in choices that we make
	- To choose between various options in home decorating
	- To illustrate and explain these choices
	- To use conjunctions appropriately
Level:	Elementary
Time:	60 minutes
Materials:	A worksheet in which students explain their décor choices in their bedrooms
Preparation:	Prepare the handout, one copy for each student.

Language practice	
Skills?	listening, writing, vocabulary, drawing
What?	finding information about interior decorating, completing room sketch, completing sentences on the worksheet
How?	searching for information online individually, sharing information and explaining choices in pairs, completing worksheet independently

Procedure

1. Explain to students that they are going to be asked to design their ideal or dream bedroom.

182

From Implications to Application

2. Ask them to draw the outline of the room, indicating where the door and windows are. Allow students time to use the internet to access home decorating sites for ideas.

3. Before giving students more explicit instructions (see later), let them discuss in pairs or small groups what their dream bedroom might look like. This will help generate some ideas.

4. Then ask students what will be the first things they need to consider:

   a. walls: paint (color), wallpaper (pattern)
   b. floor: carpet, wood, tiles
   c. lights: ceiling lights, bedside lights
   d. windows: curtains, blinds, no covering

5. Ask students to indicate their choices on the room sketch. Examples of patterns and colors can be indicated next to the sketch.

6. Students can then choose the furniture for the room.

   a. What kind of bed would you choose? Why?
   b. What kind of storage facilities do you want?
   c. What about a workspace?
   d. Do you have hobbies you would like to accommodate?

   Ask them to show all these aspects on the sketch.

7. Finally ask them to consider how they would decorate the room.

   a. Would you use photos, paintings, posters, or plants?
   b. What else would like to include in your room to decorate it?

   Ask them to indicate on the sketch where these would be placed in the room.

8. When the students have finished, ask them to complete the worksheet using their sketch to guide their answers.

9. Ask students to pair up again with their previous partner and to describe to each other their completed sketch using the answers they have written on the worksheet.

183

From Implications to Application

Extension

The students can be asked to design any room in the house or even a whole house or apartment. This could be done on a computer using appropriate drawing tools. Working in pairs to do the task will create opportunities for negotiation and decision making. If done online, the outcome could be distributed to other class members. They could in addition be shown in the form of an oral presentation.

Students could write an article about the room, explaining their choices for a lifestyle magazine. They could perhaps write a short article giving tips about design and suggesting what readers should bear in mind when decorating.

Teacher Reflection

How is your classroom organized? What does the arrangement of furniture and other objects say about you?

Think of your current classroom and circle YES or NO in response to the following statements:

1. I am happy with the way my classroom is organized. YES or NO
2. I have the authority to arrange my own classroom space. YES or NO
3. I have my own classroom. YES or NO
4. My school is happy for me to (re)arrange the furniture in my classroom. YES or NO
5. My classroom is rather colorful. YES or NO
6. My students find my classroom welcoming. YES or NO
7. Students struggle to move around the classroom. YES or NO
8. I bring a lot of my own stuff into my classroom. YES or NO
9. I feel like my classroom reflects my personality. YES or NO
10. I can be who I want to be as a teacher in my classroom. YES or NO

From Implications to Application

Materials

Worksheet

1. Complete these sentences:

    a. I painted the walls _____ *because*
        I _____.
        I used _____ wallpaper *because* _____.

    b. My favorite floor covering is _____. I like it *because*
        _____.

    c. *Because* good lighting is important in a bedroom, I chose
        _____.

    d. Seeing that I prefer _____, I used
        _____ for the windows.

2. Answer the following questions about one of the following (a) your
    storage system (b) your workspace (c) your hobby section:

    a. Why did you choose to arrange the space in this way?

    b. What was the most important thing you had to consider? Why
        was this important?

3. Select one of the items you chose to decorate your room and
    explain why it is important to you. _____

4. What does your completed room say about YOU? _____
    _____.

Activity 40: Names for (Online) Gamers

Introduction

In today's society, gaming plays a huge role in what people do in their
leisure time and has a significant impact on the way they see themselves.
'Gamer' is an identity adopted by many young people (and older ones)
who are immersed in the culture of video games. Their identity as a
gamer is reflected in their choice of gamer name. Research suggests
that some gamers consider their online names to be as important as
the ones given to them by their parents. Another issue is that it appears

185

From Implications to Application

that female gamers are not as welcome in the world of gaming as their male counterparts. This gives rise to interesting questions as to whether female gamers should reveal their gender through their choice of name. This activity asks students to reflect on gamer names by completing a worksheet and then sharing their views in pairs.

Aim	- To consider online gamer identities
	- To justify the choice of gamer names
	- To relate gamer names to personal identity
Level:	Intermediate
Time:	40 minutes
Materials:	Examples of online names and the worksheets in the Materials section
Preparation:	- Find some examples of online gamer names.
	- Photocopy worksheets for all students.

Language practice	
Skills?	listening, speaking, writing
What?	listening to class discussion, completing sentences, sharing opinions
How?	whole-class discussion, completing worksheet independently, sharing information in pairs

Procedure

1. Ask the class how many of them identify as online gamers. Ask the gamers in the class to talk about the different games that they play and why they enjoy them.

2. Then ask one or two if they are willing to share their online names and, if so, how they decided on them. Quite often these names are a version of their own names, what they are interested in (e.g., some kind of sport), or a fictional character (e.g., someone from a movie, or TV series, or a book). Sometimes gamers want to adopt frightening names such as Deathstalker. (Advise students that there

From Implications to Application

are millions of online gamers, so they might want to choose a name that is not too common. Remind them, too, that in the interests of online security, they probably don't want to give away too much personal information in their online names.)

3. You will probably have two groups of students in your class. One group will be made up of gamers and the other of learners who do not play games online.

   a. Ask those students who have an online name to think about their name. Would they choose the same name again? If so, can they explain why they are happy with the name? If not, what new name would they use? Why would they choose this name?

   b. Ask those students who do not have an online name to decide on one that they would use if they decided to play online games. Why would they choose this name?

4. Give students the worksheet. Explain it to them and then ask them to complete the relevant part of Section A. They work on this independently.

5. After they have completed Section A, ask them to pair up with a partner. In pairs, they share the information they have written on their own worksheets.

6. Again, in the same pairs, students comment on the quality of the name by completing Section B on the worksheet.

7. To end the activity, ask students to call out their (proposed) game name. Comment on how the name relates to personal identity. You could ask students to point out what the name says about who they think are.

Extension

Intermediate and advanced students could be asked to think more thoroughly about how their identities are reflected in their choice of online names. They could discuss various examples of online names and speculate as to the motivation behind the choices. Another area that could be investigated is gender discrimination, which is apparently a problem in the online environment. Girl gamers are not welcome! Students could discuss whether women playing games online should

From Implications to Application

disguise their identity or make it evident in their choice of names. Students would be asked to justify their reasoning. Exploring sites such the following could stimulate further reflection and debate: https://tocaboca.com/magazine/identity-issue_digital-life.

Teacher Reflection

1. In this activity, many students will have revealed their real or potential gamer names. Do you think the names say something about the identity of the students? Has it perhaps changed your opinion of any of them?
2. If your students were to assign you a gamer name, what possible names would they choose? Why is this the case?
3. Would these names be similar to names your teacher colleagues might give you?

Materials

Worksheets

Section A

Answer these questions if you already have an online name:

1. What is your online name?

2. Why did you choose this name?

    a. I chose this name because _____

3. Are you still happy with your choice?

    a. Yes, I am because _____

    b. No, I would change it because _____

4. What advice would you give to someone choosing a name for the first time?

    a. I would advise them to _____ because _____

188

From Implications to Application

Answer these questions if you do not have an online name:

1. What online name would you choose?

2. Why would you choose this name?

   a. I would choose this name because _____

3. If this name was not available, what other name would you choose?

   a. I would choose _____ because

   _____

4. Why did you choose this name, and what advice would you give to someone choosing a name for the first time?

   a. I chose this name because _____

   b. I would advise them to _____ because _____

Section B

I think this is a good or bad name because _____

Activity 41: The Aliens Have Landed

Introduction

We are fascinated by the unknown, and the concept of alien life has always stirred people's imagination. In this light-hearted activity, students are asked to imagine and then describe an alien life form they would like to be ('an ideal alien') to a listener who will draw the alien from the description provided. The students are encouraged to use their own imaginations and be creative!

Aim:	- To use descriptive adjectives
	- To give clear instructions
	- To listen carefully
Level:	Elementary
Time:	50 minutes

189

From Implications to Application

Materials: Cartoon pictures of alien life forms, colored pencils or markers

Preparation: There are numerous examples of simple cartoon drawings of aliens online. Be prepared to draw one yourself to show students how easy it is.

Language practice	
Skills?	speaking, listening, vocabulary
What?	giving instructions on how to draw an alien, following instructions to reproduce a drawing, using appropriate adjectives
How?	class discussion, drawing a picture individually, working in pairs

Procedure

1. Start a discussion with students about outer space and life that might exist there. Talk about the various forms that people imagine aliens can take.
2. Draw your own alien on the board, explaining to students that this is a light-hearted exercise. Give your alien an identity and describe it to the students. Write a number of simple adjectives on the board that describe your alien's identity.
3. Distribute the colored pencils and ask students to draw the alien they would like to be. In other words, they draw how they would like to see themselves as an alien—*an ideal alien*. Stress that it can be any shape or form they like and consist of any colors or patterns. Ask them not to show their drawings to their classmates.
4. Randomly pair up students. One student, without showing the partner the drawing, describes it in detail, including its colors, shape, and so on. At the same time, the other student listens carefully and attempts to replicate the original drawing. Instructions would be similar to:

    a. Draw a square.
    b. Put a circle on top.

From Implications to Application

c. Color the circle blue.

d. Add a face with one red eye inside the circle, and so on.

5. After the drawing has been completed, the students switch roles, with the first drawer now giving instructions so the partner can draw their alien.

6. After the pairs compare the two drawings, the class (or larger groups) then compares each set of two drawings to see which two are most alike.

7. Ask students to write a number of adjectives they used or heard others using to describe what their aliens look like next to the drawing of their alien.

8. They then add three further adjectives that describe the character (or identity) of the alien (e.g., nasty, powerful, evil, kind, sexy).

9. In pairs, they explain why they assigned those identity features. How do these features relate to themselves—to their own identities? Why did they choose to imagine themselves as that kind of alien?

Extension

This lesson can be approached in different ways. More advanced students can draw maps of where the aliens live, which their partners have to replicate. Students can also attempt to replicate patterns. They can also be given photos that they must describe to their partners. Students might use an identikit option where they describe another person who they must then draw.

Teacher Reflection

Imagine you could teach anywhere in the world—any place, any students, any conditions.

1. Where would it be? Why—what makes the place appealing?
2. Who would your students be? Why—what makes them appealing?

191

From Implications to Application

> 3. What conditions of work would you choose (e.g., salary, work-load)? Why?
>
> What do your choices in 1 to 3 say about you as a professional language teacher?

Activity 42: Speaking English Tomorrow

Introduction

This activity requires students to complete a narrative frame—a short story template with sentence starters and blank spaces to write in. Students need to imagine an occasion when they will speak English the following day, who they will speak to, and what the outcome of the interaction might be. The activity gives the students the opportunity to imagine a future event in which they will speak English, who they will encounter during the interaction, and what the linguistic and identity-related consequences of that interaction might be.

Aim:	- To imagine a future oriented speaking interaction
	- To anticipate language problems
	- To negotiate identity with an imagined interlocutor
	- To practice writing a coherent paragraph
Level:	Intermediate
Time:	50 minutes
Materials:	A narrative frame for each student
Preparation:	- Print a copy of the narrative frame for each student.
	- Complete the frame yourself to experience what your learners will do.

192

From Implications to Application

Language practice	
Skills?	writing, speaking, reading aloud
What?	imagining the future, making comparisons, expressing an emotion
How?	completing frame independently, comparing responses in groups, reading to whole class, whole-class discussion, pair work

Procedure

1. Provide each student with a copy of the narrative frame.
2. Explain to students how to complete the frame: (a) read the blank frame in full, (b) fill in the blank spaces, (c) write a coherent story.
3. Allow enough time for all students to finish the frame (about 15 minutes)
4. In groups of three or four, students consider the responses to each of the six starters in turn and do the following:

   a. Describe how the imagined speaking events are *similar* and *different*.
   b. Describe the characteristics of the people involved in the interactions. Generate a list adjectives.
   c. Identify the imagined speaking problem in each case. Provide one keyword for each problem.
   d. Provide one emotion word (e.g., happy, scared, satisfied) that describes each response to the final starter.

5. Ask two or three student volunteers to read their frames to the class.
6. After each reading, highlight any instances of identity categorization referred to in the frames (e.g., native speaker, gender, ethnicity, nationality) and write these as a keyword (e.g., English speaker, female, Indian, Malaysian) on the board.
7. For a few minutes, encourage students to ask questions about the keywords and engage them in a discussion of identity in relation to the imagined language use described in the frames. Use questions such as: How do you see yourself? How do you want

193

From Implications to Application

to be seen? How do other people see you? What do other people think about you? How does this make you feel?

8. Students then, in pairs (different members from their group), share their answers to b, c, and d in 4, writing down at least three different:

- imagined language problems keywords
- emotion words

Teacher Reflection

Imagine your own linguistic interactions *tomorrow* (e.g., while shopping, eating a meal, making a phone call, participating in a school meeting):

1. Who will they probably be with?
2. What language(s) will you predominantly use?
3. How will the interactions make you feel?
4. Can you transfer any of these experiences to your classroom teaching? How?

Materials

The Narrative Frame

Tomorrow I will speak English outside of the classroom when (give one example) _____

_____

_____

_____. I know this will happen because _____

_____. The person I will speak to is _____

_____

_____. I may have a problem with _____

_____

_____. However, I know that _____

_____

And I will feel _____.

194

From Implications to Application

Activity 43: Identity Quotes

Introduction

This activity introduces students to famous English quotes about identity. Students are asked to decide which of these quotes resonates most with them. They then paraphrase selected quote and explain how they would present this quote on a poster. Students discuss their different approaches to the presentation in groups.

Aim:	- To introduce students to highly regarded identity quotes
	- To paraphrase these quotes
	- To discuss how they believe this quote could be presented in the form of a poster
Level:	Intermediate
Time:	60 minutes
Materials:	Bring one or more quotes of your choice about identity to class. Pictures of posters illustrating these quotes (these could be on the internet). A worksheet is provided.
Preparation:	Prepare a copy of the worksheet for each student.

Language practice	
Skills?	speaking, paraphrasing, writing
What?	putting quotes into own words (paraphrasing), explaining how to best present quotes, comparing opinions, writing a short paragraph
How?	whole-class discussions, group discussions, completing worksheet individually

Procedure

1. Discuss the concept of identity with students. Quite often the words of others help us express what we are feeling. On the worksheet are six quotes on identity that go some way towards achieving this.

195

From Implications to Application

2. Read the quotes with the students. Ask them which one they like best. Did any of the quotes resonate with how they see themselves now or who they would one day like to be?
3. Facilitate a class discussion on the quotes and what students understand them to mean. One way of doing this might be to get students who have chosen the same quote to discuss among themselves what they think the quote means. They might find that they have very different opinions. Again, ask them if they see themselves in the quote.
4. Then talk to students about paraphrasing. What is it? Why do we use it? Why is it important in writing? Put up the quote you brought with you to the class and ask students to help you to paraphrase it. Students might want to make use of thesauruses and online dictionaries. Remember though to stress that a paraphrase seeks to capture the meaning and should never just be a case of substituting one word for another.
5. Then ask students to complete the worksheet individually.
6. After the students have completed the worksheet, ask them to get into groups with students who have chosen the same best quote. Let them look at how each student has chosen to present the quote in a poster. They might want to compare different rationales.
7. Ask each student, still in groups, to take a turn to explain to the other students their personal connection to their quote and poster.

    a. How does it make them feel?
    b. Does it motivate them in any way?
    c. Does the quote reflect who they are?
    d. Or who they want to be?

Extension

Advanced students could be asked to find their own quotes about identity and explain their reasons for choosing them. These students might also look for identity quotes in their own languages and compare them with the quotes in English. Do different cultural groups appear to highlight different aspects of identity?

From Implications to Application

There are also many English quotes on identity from books aimed at children or young adults. The Dr. Seuss quote in this activity is an example. You can find these types of quotes online. They are usually easier to understand than those quotes aimed at adults, so they might be suitable for learners at the elementary level.

Teacher Reflection

Read the following five quotes. How do they resonate with you—your identity and your practice?

1. "Teaching is a very noble profession that shapes the character, caliber, and future of an individual. If the people remember me as a good teacher, that will be the biggest honour for me."—A.P.J. Abdul Kalam
2. "A good teacher, like a good entertainer first must hold his audience's attention, then he can teach his lesson."—John Henrik Clarke
3. "The greatest sign of success for a teacher . . . is to be able to say, 'The children are now working as if I did not exist.'"—Maria Montessori
4. "I have learned that, although I am a good teacher, I am a much better student, and I was blessed to learn valuable lessons from my students on a daily basis. They taught me the importance of teaching to a student—and not to a test."—Erin Gruwell
5. "So what does a good teacher do? Create tension—but just the right amount."—Donald Norman

Source: www.brainyquote.com/topics/teacher

Materials

Worksheet

The following are quotes about identity. When you have read them answer the questions below.

197

From Implications to Application

a. "Be who you are and say what you feel because those who mind don't matter and those who matter don't mind."—Dr. Seuss
b. "One of the greatest tragedies in life is to lose your own sense of self and accept the version of you that is expected by everyone else."—K.L. Toth
c. "Unlike a drop of water which loses its identity when it joins the ocean, man does not lose his being in the society in which he lives. Man's life is independent. He is born not for the development of the society alone, but for the development of his self."—B.R. Ambedkar
d. "So, I guess we are who we are for a lot of reasons. And maybe we'll never know most of them. But even if we don't have the power to choose where we come from, we can still choose where we go from there. We can still do things. And we can try to feel okay about them."—Stephen Chbosky
e. "Life is about creating yourself."—George Bernard Shaw
f. "Never mind searching for who you are. Search for the person you aspire to be."—Robert Brault

1. Which quote did you like the most? Why?
2. Rewrite the quote *in your own words*. Try to capture the author's meaning.
3. Often quotes like these are printed on posters that people display to remind themselves of what is important to them. Look at your quote. If you were to turn it into a poster, what would the poster look like? Think about the following:

- Would you have a photo or picture on the poster? What kind of photo or picture would you choose? Would you perhaps just use colors or patterns?
- Where would you put the quote on the poster? How big would the letters be? What color(s) would you use?
- What shape would the poster be? How would you hang it on a wall?
- Who do you think the poster would appeal to (e.g., students, activists, old or young people)?

From Implications to Application

4. Make a simple sketch of how you would like the poster to look.
5. Finally, write a short paragraph explaining your choices about how you would display your poster (see point 3).

Activity 44: Different Perspectives

Introduction

How we report what we see and hear often depends on our prejudices. For example, parents with young children might view the behavior of their own children very differently from people who don't have children. Parents might see behavior as cute or funny, whereas others might see it as rude and undisciplined. It is a good idea to be aware of our own prejudices and to be aware that people don't necessarily see things the way we do! In this activity, students read a short text and write two newspaper reports on it, from two different perspectives.

Aim:	- To identify ways to report an incident from different perspectives
	- To identify the kinds of words that represent these perspectives
	- To write a short newspaper article
Level:	Intermediate
Time:	60 minutes
Materials:	One worksheet consisting of written text
Preparation:	Prepare one copy of the worksheet for each student.

Language practice	
Skills?	reading, writing
What?	reading factual information, vocabulary to express differing perspectives, writing a short newspaper report
How?	silent reading, group work, writing independently

199

From Implications to Application

Procedure

1. Provide students with the worksheet and allow them an opportunity to read through the text silently.
2. In groups ask them to identify *silly* and *sensible* things the group did, for example:

   - Silly: They left quite late in the afternoon in winter. They should have realized it would get dark quite soon.
   - Sensible: They all had warm, weather-proof coats.

3. The local newspaper wants to publish a short account of the incident.
4. Ask the students to write two brief reports (give them an appropriate word limit):

   a. the first report from the perspective of a young person who is friendly with the four teenagers involved
   b. the second report by an older person, a volunteer who spends a lot of time looking after the bush walks and who was part of the search party

5. Tell the class they are free to report as they wish, but they cannot change the facts.
6. They should write a headline for each of the reports.
7. When the class has finished, ask them to compare the different accounts in pairs, focusing on the following questions:

   a. What was highlighted in the teenagers' report?
   b. What did the older person concentrate on?
   c. Why do you think they made these choices?
   d. What do the two versions of the report tell you about the identities of the younger and older person? (This questions could be used for whole-class discussion to wrap up the activity.)

Extension

Any incident reported in a local (online) newspaper could be adopted for this exercise. An extension would be to find the reporting of the

From Implications to Application

same incident in different sources. Students could be asked to compare and contrast the different reporting styles and then asked if they could identify where the writers' sympathies lie. They can be asked to identify keywords that support their views.

> **Teacher Reflection**
>
> Is there potentially an exploratory action research project (see Part 4) for you stemming from this activity?
>
> An interesting topic might be to explore how, when, and in which languages your students engage with news media—(online) newspapers, Twitter, podcasts—and how it relates to their perceptions of their language learning. You could develop a short survey to distribute to your students and follow up with individual interviews or classroom discussion. The findings of the study might give you good ideas for how to incorporate news media into your lessons. Would this be a good idea?

Materials

Worksheet

On June 2, 2018, at 3:00 pm, Jane Phillips (16), Jason Fraser (17), Jennifer Marshall (17) and Peter Woodburn (18) left the holiday accommodation where they were staying in New Zealand to go for a walk through the bush. They followed a trail that had been recommended to them by the hotel manager. They were all wearing jeans, T-shirts, and warm rainproof jackets. They refused an offer of a radio as they said they had their iPhones. They told the manager that they would be back by 6. The group missed one of the track signs and got lost in the bush. After walking for approximately two hours, they came across a hut that was used to accommodate hikers on the Golden Valley Track. The hut was locked because the track is not open to hikers in winter. The group broke a window to get into the hut. The group then used an axe that was stored in the hut to chop branches off trees in the

From Implications to Application

vicinity so that they could make a fire. The group was found the next day by a search party that had spent the night looking for them.

Activity 45: What Makes Them Them?

Introduction

In this activity, learners construct an identity for a stranger using visual clues. They write descriptions of people depicted in pictures and then compare their descriptions with students who independently wrote about the same person. (If the students completed *Activity 3: What Makes Me Me?* they could will revisit the collages they created to remind themselves of the diffuse layers that make up our identities.)

Aim:	- To use visual clues to construct an identity
	- To write a short description of a person depicted in a picture, commenting on their identity
	- To share and compare their description with other students
Level:	Intermediate
Time:	60 minutes
Materials:	Pictures (photos, paintings, magazine cut-outs, digital photos from the internet) of people from a wide range of life, in particular, pictures that show the whole person and the background. People can be models or better still simply pictures of ordinary people. The photos should not include celebrities.
Preparation:	- Prepare enough pictures so that each student receives one.
	- Students could also be asked before the lesson to bring photos of different people.
	- Photocopy each picture so that you have two copies per picture.

202

From Implications to Application

Language practice	
Skills?	listening, visual literacy, writing, speaking
What?	analyzing details in a picture, weighing their significance, writing a short description, comparing and justifying written descriptions
How?	whole-class discussion, writing independently, comparing in pairs

Procedure

1. Using one photo as an example, ask the students to look for clues in the photo that give more information about the person. There are obvious markers such as gender and age but students can also consider the following:

   - Look at clothing. Does the person seem to be poor or wealthy?
   - Are there religious markers (e.g., crosses or a distinctive way of dressing)?
   - Students can see whether someone appears to belong to a specific ethnicity. Talk about the person's body. What does this tell us about them?
   - And the person's face? Do they look happy, sad, contented, excited, resigned, angry?
   - The background can also give us clues about the person. Was the photo taken where the person is surrounded by other people? Is the person alone?
   - Are there animals in the picture? Was the photo taken outside? Is the person on holiday or at a pollical rally? Does she or he appear to be at work?

2. After the discussion, give out the photos, making sure that two students get the same photo but ensure that they do not sit together.
3. Ask students to write a short description of the person using the visual clues and focusing on their identity. Who do they imagine the person to be?

From Implications to Application

4. Allow the students enough time to write about the person in their photo. Students need to explain why they have attributed certain characteristics to the photo. For example:

   I think she is sad. She has deep lines next to her mouth, and her eyes don't have any life. There are photos of children on the wall dressed in clothes that were fashionable a long time ago. Perhaps they have left home, and she is lonely.

5. The amount you ask students to write will depend on their ability and the amount of time available.
6. After they have finished their descriptions, ask the students who shared the same photo to get together and compare their descriptions. Students should find it interesting to see if they are similar or different. Ask them to look at the various reasons they give for the selection of details in their descriptions.

Teacher Reflection

This activity might help students develop greater empathy for others. It might offer an opportunity to explore beneath the superficial and try to walk in someone else's shoes. But what about you?

Think about the visual clues in your classroom while you are teaching:

1. Which are the most salient, those that typically attract your attention?
2. What finer details might you be missing?
3. How do these clues help you understand your students— who they are, the lives they lead outside the classroom?
4. Does this understanding contribute to the nature of your relationship with your students?

In future classes, try to pay particular attention to the visual clues that are more and less obvious.

204

From Implications to Application

Activity 46: Social Justice and Advertising

Introduction

Advertising is not just used for commercial reasons. Ads can also be used to promote social justice issues, such as raising environmental concerns, persuading people not to drink and drive, and highlighting racism and sexism. In this activity, students identify social issues that resonate with themselves. They analyze ads about causes that interest them and discuss their effectiveness.

Aim:	- To examine the information and language in ads - To work in groups to discuss the choice of information - To examine the effectiveness of the language - To compare and contrast divergent views
Level:	Advanced
Time:	60 minutes
Materials:	Ads about social issues downloaded from the internet or extracted from magazines or newspapers. A worksheet is provided.
Preparation:	- Find ads that cover a variety of social issues. - Prepare copies of each ad and bring enough to ensure that students will have some choice. - Prepare copies of the worksheets.

Language practice	
Skills?	speaking, visual literacy
What?	researching and evaluating information in ads, commenting on their effectiveness
How?	class discussions, group work, completing worksheets in groups

205

From Implications to Application

Procedure

1. Discuss the use of ads to promote social justice issues. The students will be familiar with slogans such as:

   a. Save paper—save the planet.
   b. For the homeless, every day is a struggle.
   c. Your skin color shouldn't dictate your future.

2. On the board, write down the issues represented in the ads you have brought to class (e.g., drug abuse, homelessness, child poverty). Ask the students what kind of people might be interested in such ads—what people would sympathize with the causes? In other words, ask them to imagine the identities of the people engaging with the ads and what their responses to the ads might be. Also, ask them to reflect on what *their own* personal responses are. How do their identities react to the ads?

3. Ask students to choose one of the issues that they feel strongly about and then form a group with other students who share the same interest.

4. Give each group the ad or ads that match their interest.

5. In their groups, students discuss the social issue they have selected and analyze the ad(s).

   a. They look at the visuals and the information presented.
   b. They then use the internet to check the information in the ad.
   c. They read more widely to gain a deeper understanding of the issue. For example, if they are looking at homelessness that might look at how this plays out in particular countries or how it affects people of different ages, genders, or ethnicities.

6. In the course of their research, ask students to look for photographs or pictures that they believe might be effective in this kind of ad.

7. After the students have had sufficient time to explore their topic, hand out the worksheet, one to each group.

8. The students will then complete the worksheet in their groups.

206

From Implications to Application

9. After they have completed the worksheets, facilitate a class discussion about the ads.

    a. Ask students to focus in particular on the kinds of information that they think will be effective in putting the message across and the way in which such information could be delivered.
    b. Ask them to consider the link between the visual material and the language used.
    c. What audience would specifically be targeted? What kind of people (imagined identities) would the advertisers be wanting to influence? How would they want to change them?

Extension

Extension work for this lesson could be to ask students to actually design a social issues ad using the material that they have already collected. This can be done in groups or individually in a follow-up lesson.

Teacher Reflection

Consider these questions:

1. Do you believe it is the responsibility of language teachers to raise social issues with language learners?
2. Do you believe that the classroom is a place to encourage discussion of these issues?
3. How do you handle differences of opinion on major social issues?
4. Do you think you should remain neutral or should you make your opinion known?

Material

Worksheet

1. What is the social issue highlighted?
2. What is the reader told about this issue?

207

From Implications to Application

3. Do you think the ad is effective?

   a. Why or why not?

4. What other information do you think should or could be presented? Remember that this information would have to be presented very succinctly.
5. Have you found any statistics that you think could be used effectively in an advertising campaign?

   a. What are they?
   b. How could they be effectively presented?

6. What about the visual material presented in the ad?

   a. Do you think it is effective?
   b. Have you found other photographs or pictures that you think could also be used?

Activity 47: Consumer Identity

Introduction

Consumer identity has become increasingly important in modern society. We do not just buy something because of its functional use. We use brands and products to express our identities. It is therefore very important that retailers understand what people value. Why is one product that fulfils the same function more desirable than another? In this activity, students examine how product slogans are designed to appeal to what people want to be, for example, sophisticated, intelligent, or sincere. Students analyze various slogans in groups and then individually choose what they consider to be the best and least successful slogans, justifying their choices.

Aim:
- To reflect on identity and consumerism
- To categorize well-known English slogans using distinctions employed by the advertising industry

208

From Implications to Application

- To identify the audience at which they are aimed
- To evaluate how effective the slogans are

Level: Advanced

Time: 60 minutes

Materials: A worksheet with the slogans and explanations of the categories

Preparation:
- Find a number of well know slogans not on the worksheet to initiate a class discussion.
- Prepare copies of the worksheet as presented below for each student.

Language practice	
Skills?	listening, speaking, specialized vocabulary
What?	listening to instruction, analyzing slogans, debating, justifying choices
How?	whole-class discussion, working in groups and individually to complete the worksheet

Procedure

1. Initiate a class discussion about why we buy what we buy. Ask students to consider why one pair of sports shoes is more appealing than another if they both do the same job. What influences our choices about what we buy? Researchers believe that what consumers are looking for is a match between the brand they are buying and their own self-image, who they imagine themselves to be, or who they desire to be. Often marketers will give brands human-like characteristics in order to give them appeal to different consumers. Market researchers believe that there are five broad categories:

    a. down to earth (sincere, honest, wholesome, and cheerful)
    b. exciting (daring, imaginative, and up to date)
    c. successful (reliable, intelligent, and competent)

209

From Implications to Application

    d.   sophisticated (glamorous, wealthy, charming)

    e.   tough (outdoorsy and rugged)

2.   Write the categories on the board.

3.   Ask students what they think about this categorization. The following are some possible questions:

    a.   What influences them the most when they buy different items?

    b.   Does the motivation differ when they are buying different kinds of items (e.g., clothes, food, cleaning items)?

    c.   How does what they buy relate to who they desire to be?

    d.   What's the connection between product and person (consumer)?

4.   Ask the class to come up with well know slogans—both in their own language and in English. Write them on the board and discuss why these particular slogans have become so famous. What is it about the words that appeals to people? Are the ads aimed at a particular group of people, or are they designed to have general appeal?

5.   Then divide the class into groups.

6.   Hand out the worksheets, one to each student.

7.   Ask them to complete the worksheets initially in groups (Part A) and later individually (Part B).

8.   If time allows, students compare their answers to the last question on the worksheet in their groups. Ask them to consider the following question in relation to the four selected slogans in Part B: *How do these slogans relate to me—who I think I am and who I imagine myself to be?*

Extension

Students working in groups could be asked to imagine an item (e.g., a pair of shoes, a new chocolate, a soft drink). They could then be asked to decide which of the five categories listed they would choose to use (justifying their choice). They must then compose a slogan for this imaginary product. Elementary students could be given well known slogans and asked to identify the product. They could use the internet to help them.

210

From Implications to Application

> **Teacher Reflection**
>
> Slogans aren't only evident or visible in advertising. We find them in businesses, corporations, and other professional environments such as educational institutions. Have you noticed any slogans in:
>
> a. your school
> b. your educational system
> c. materials and other resources you use in the classroom
> d. professional associations you belong to
>
> How do these slogans relate to who you think *you are* as a teacher, or who you *would like to be*?

Materials

Worksheet

Part A: Group Work

The five categories identified by the advertising industry are:

1. down to earth (sincere, honest, wholesome, and cheerful)
2. exciting (daring, imaginative, and up to date)
3. successful (reliable, intelligent, and competent)
4. sophisticated (glamorous, wealthy, charming)
5. tough (outdoorsy and rugged)

Read the slogans below. Which of these five categories do they belong to? Write 1 to 5 in the Category column. Who do you think the slogans are aimed at (e.g., a general audience, athletes, young people)?

Slogan	Category	Audience
There are some things money can't buy. For everything else, there's MasterCard. (MasterCard)		

211

From Implications to Application

Slogan	Category	Audience
Melts in your mouth, not in your hands. (M&M).		
Just do it. (Nike)		
Think different. (Apple)		
Because you're worth it. (L'Oreal Paris)		
Quality never goes out of style. (Levi's)		
Have a break. Have a Kit Kat. (Kit Kat)		
Advancement through technology. (Audi)		
Open happiness. (Coke)		
Impossible is nothing. (Adidas)		
Money to burn but the good sense not to. (Hyundai)		
Eat fresh. (Subway)		

Part B: Individual Work

Slogans are key phrases or sets of words that capture the essence of a brand. Slogans need to stick in the minds of consumers. A good slogan:

- is usually short, catchy, and easy to remember
- highlights what is good about a product or service
- gives potential buyers a positive feeling or incentive
- tells buyers why a product is different or unique

    a.   Which two slogans above do you think are the best ones? Why do you think so?

From Implications to Application

b. Which two do you think are least successful? Why do you think so?

c. Compare your answers with other group members.

Information sourced from:

Aaker, J. (1997). Dimensions of brand personality. *Journal of Marketing Research*, *34*(3), 347–356. Retrieved from https://econsultancy.com/what-makes-an-effective-brand-slogan/

Activity 48: Transport of the Future

Introduction

We all use some form of transport, either public or private. These different forms of transport are increasingly coming under scrutiny because of their impact on the environment. For many of us, getting around can be a real hassle, although some lucky people enjoy their chosen mode of transport. In this activity, students consider their own preferred modes of transport, how their choices reflect their identities, and how transport might change in the future.

Aim:	- To discuss current forms of transport used by students
	- To identify the pros and cons of this transport
	- To read a passage on forms of transport in the future
	- To complete a worksheet on the advantages and disadvantages of new proposals
Level:	Advanced
Time:	60 minutes
Materials:	A worksheet on different modes of transport is provided.
Preparation:	- Students might find some of the ideas introduced in the passage difficult to envisage (e.g., a straddling bus, self-driving pods, zip-line commute).

213

From Implications to Application

Illustrations of these proposed new modes of transport can be found online.
- Prepare copies of the worksheet as presented for each student.

Language practice	
Skills?	reading and comprehension, speaking
What?	reading a comprehension passage, weighing up pros and cons
How?	whole-class and group discussion, silent reading individually, completing worksheets in pairs or small groups

Procedure

1. Start the class by discussing with students what kind of transport they use and how this choice of transport might reflect who they are—their views on climate change and their socioeconomic status, for example.

   - How do you get to school or college?
   - How do you get to your social activities?
   - Why do you choose these means of transport? Why not other types of transport, which may be faster or more comfortable?

   Then ask students to talk about some of the advantages and disadvantages associated with the different forms of transport they mention.

2. Then ask students to think about how transport is changing. Students discuss in groups:

   a. What are some of the major changes?
   b. Why is transport changing? (You could suggest, e.g., climate change, cost, advances in technology.)
   c. How do these changes affect your life?
   d. Do you support them?

From Implications to Application

3. Give students copies of the worksheet to read. They can do this silently by themselves.
4. After they have read the passage, ask them to think about the advantages and disadvantages of each of the proposed systems and fill in the worksheet in pairs or small groups.
5. Then students choose one of the proposed forms of transport they would most like to see introduced in their home environment, giving reasons to justify their choice. In discussing these together as a whole class, encourage students to reflect on how their choice of transport relates to themselves (e.g., their personal and family backgrounds, their social experiences, their views of progress and sustainability).

Teacher Reflection

Consider these questions:

1. Do you know how transport currently affects your students' lives? Does it affect their learning in any way?
2. What about you? Does transport affect your professional life in any way?
   - getting to work and back home
   - the financial burden
   - attending extra-curricular events
   - attending meetings and professional development workshops or conferences
   - too time consuming

Materials

Transport of the Future

How do you get around? Do you rely on public transport, or do you have a car, motorbike, or scooter? Perhaps you rely on your own power to get around (e.g., you walk or you have a pushbike). Probably you rely on a number of different options. If you live in a big city, though, it is likely

From Implications to Application

that getting around is becoming increasingly difficult. Traffic jams don't just occur in rush hours, but roads can be congested all day long. Not only are these delays frustrating and time wasting for millions of people, traditional forms of transport also contribute to pollution in big cities.

Fortunately, scientists are coming up with new technologies to address the problems. One of the most popular is the so-called hyper loop, which consists of pod-like carriages on a track. These carriages will be able to travel more than 100 km an hour and will be able to transport cargo as well as people.

Another interesting concept that has actually been built and tested in China is the straddling bus. This electric bus has been designed so that cars can drive underneath it—it straddles the road. The bus does need a special track on either side of the roadway, but developers say it will be much cheaper than building a subway line.

Another concept that scientists are developing is the never-stopping train. One of the things that slows down train journeys is stopping at each station. Researchers have come up with the idea of a never-stopping train. This train looks pretty much like an ordinary train, but it has coaches on top of the ones on the tracks. When the train comes into a station, people who want to get off move to the carriages on top. These carriages are then able to detach from the train when it comes into the station. Similarly, people who want to get onto the train will be waiting in carriages at the station that will then attach to the top of the train. After this has happened, then people can move down into the main carriages. In this way, the train will never have to stop at stations.

It's not just traveling in cities that is a problem—sometimes the terrain means that trips can be very long. Norway has 1100 fjords, and most people rely on a network of ferries to travel, but they are time consuming and inconvenient. Now, the country is developing submerged floating bridges. These bridges will be suspended 100 feet below the water's surface and will be wide enough for two lanes of traffic. At this depth, the bridges will not interfere with shipping and will be sheltered from the weather. They will be anchored to the ocean floor below.

From Implications to Application

There have also been developments as far as individual transport is concerned. Engineers are convinced that in 10 years' time, a great many of the transport systems will not require drivers. They believe that we will have evolved past self-driving cars, and we will be using self-driving pods. People will summon these pods using their phones and will then be taken to their destinations.

Cyclists will also be part of exciting developments with cities planning elevated cycle paths above the city streets. This will make cycling a lot safer and more convenient and will also reduce congestion on roads. Xiamen in South East China has already constructed a 7.6-km cycle path about 5 m above the ground. Future plans include enclosing the cycle paths so that cyclists can ride all year round in pleasant controlled conditions.

The next option is not for the fainthearted. A zip-line commute is being envisaged. Martin Angelov who came up with the idea envisages a network of wires criss-crossing the skies above cities. This would enable people to zip from one place to another. Travelers using the system would fasten themselves into a battery-powered seat suspended from a steel wire and go whizzing along to their destination.

Worksheet

Mode of transport	Advantages	Disadvantages
Car	Allows independent movement Always available Private	Can be expensive to run Traffic jams waste time and fuel Not environmentally friendly
Train		
Bus		

From Implications to Application

Mode of transport	Advantages	Disadvantages
Motorbike		
Ferry		
Walking		
Bicycle		
E-bicycle		
E-scooter		
Straddling bus		
Never-stopping train		
Submerged floating bridges		
Self-driving pods		
Elevated cycle paths		
Zip-line commute		

Part 3

From Application to Implementation

A. Introduction

In Part 2, we presented 48 activities, all geared toward exploring, developing, and imagining various facets of learner identity. The next question is how these learning activities can be implemented in classrooms in different teaching contexts. Many of you will be following a prescribed curriculum in which desired learning outcomes have already been defined by an educational system or by your institution. Any curriculum is influenced by the society in which it is planned and developed; the policies and norms of the educational institution in which it is implemented; and, of course, teachers' beliefs about, understanding of, and insights into their learners (Graves, 2008). In the first part of the book, we acknowledged that even though teachers might not always agree with what is included in a nationally or institutionally prescribed curriculum, they nevertheless have to work according to its principles and guidelines.

If you feel your curriculum is prescriptive you might be wondering how you can utilize the activities in Part 2 in your particular teaching context. Bear in mind that no curriculum, no matter how well constructed, can ever come anywhere close to matching the importance of what the teacher actually does in the classroom. Part 3 begins by briefly overviewing some characteristics of the concept of curriculum and then provides suggestions for how the activities in Part 2 can be implemented within your curriculum context. We hope that the discussion and suggestions in this part will provide a springboard for your creativity and give you practical ideas for incorporating the activities into your teaching—that is, what you actually do in the classroom.

219

From Application to Implementation

B. Organization of Part 3

In Section C, we briefly discuss some characteristics of a curriculum, which we will revisit when we address implementing the activities in Section E. In Section D, we consider what you need to know in order to select activities that best suit your goals and particular teaching and learning contexts, and that will be of the greatest benefit to your learners. Putting these activities into practice in your classrooms is the focus of Section E, and the final section (Section F) makes recommendations for what to do after teaching the activities.

C. Characteristics of the Curriculum

The curriculum policy document is often referred to as the *planned* curriculum (Wette, 2009). This planned curriculum must be turned into an *instructional* curriculum (Wette, 2009), that is, what actually happens in the classroom. The teacher has to decide how the curriculum will be translated into teachable units, and how these units will be arranged.

Ylimaki (2013) identifies five dimensions of the curriculum. The first two, *intended* and *enacted*, correspond with Wette's concepts of planned and instructional curriculum, respectively. Ylimaki also specifies the *assessed* dimension, acknowledging that assessment policies and procedures play an important role in the curriculum. Ylimaki's fourth dimension refers to curriculum outcomes, what she calls the *learned* dimension. Finally, Ylimaki discusses the dimension known as the *hidden* curriculum, which deserves our close attention, particularly given the identity focus of this book.

With regard to the learned dimension, Ylimaki highlights an important aspect of teaching. While we can interpret the planned curriculum as carefully as possible and devise interesting activities that we believe will appeal to our students, we cannot really control what they actually learn. For example, the intention of the lesson might be to show learners the difference between various tenses. To contextualize the instruction and make it interesting, a teacher might decide to show how car ownership in China has changed over the years. What the teacher hopes learners

220

From Application to Implementation

will take away from the lesson is how the past, present, and present perfect tenses are used in English.

However, it is entirely possible that the learners will not remember much about tenses but will instead remember information about car ownership in China. While we do want to increase our students' general knowledge, we would probably not consider the lesson to be a great success if the students learned nothing about tenses! As Ylimaki points out, we want to minimize the gap between what is taught and what students take out of the lesson. This is where you come in — the activities in Part 2 are representative of the *planned* or *intended* dimensions of the curriculum, but they become *enacted* when you give them life in the reality of your actual classroom.

While any significant variance between what students actually learn and what we want them to learn can be very frustrating, the enactment of the hidden dimension of the curriculum is less visible and has the potential to be far more damaging to learners.

According to Ylimaki, students learn a great deal from what is not intentionally taught or not taught at all. The hidden curriculum goes beyond the classroom and encompasses the ways in which educational systems and institutions are structured and the way in which daily educational routines play out. In the school environment, a good example is the way in which sports results are reported. In co-educational (mixed gender) schools, it is often the boys' sports results that are reported before the girls' results. Over time this can give students the message that boys' achievements are more important than girls'. In a language classroom, if the only cultures that are discussed are those of so-called English-speaking countries, then it is possible that the message learners will receive is that these are the only cultures that matter.

In this regard, the most well-intentioned approaches to teaching can have unintended consequences. Harison (2008) tells of a class of refugee English learners in New Zealand. Materials that were of interest to the class were hard to come by, so some of the teachers took on the extra

221

From Application to Implementation

responsibility of developing worksheets that they thought would be more interesting for the students. Harison analyzed one of these worksheets entitled *A Success Story* and was deeply disturbed by the message implicit in the text. The text tried to engage the readers by encouraging them to identify with the main character. Unfortunately, the emphasis was on what the person could not do—read and write English. Her nationality and background were treated as unimportant. She was presented as a passive recipient of New Zealand goodwill whose greatest attribute was that she managed to please her teachers and eventually her employer. Her job (the 'success' of the story) was a menial position as a cafeteria worker. What refugee students might take away from the text was that they were unlikely to be successful in their new country and that the most they could hope for was part-time, unskilled work. Even this small 'success' would depend on their being liked by others. This is certainly not the kind of identity we wish our students to see as their lot.

As indicated in this example, the term 'hidden syllabus' often has a negative connation and is usually associated with race or gender bias. However, Hadfield (2018) argues that hidden or covert syllabuses might well have a positive role to play in learning. She gives the example of learning activities that promote group cohesion in the classroom. These activities engender feelings of group identity and pride in shared achievements and therefore have a dual goal of language learning and group building. The language learning goals are shared with students, but it would be counterproductive, Hadfield notes, to inform them that the lesson was also aimed at making them more empathetic! While this book obviously does not seek to hide its focus on identity, we concur that language learning and the exploration of identity can be a "twin progression" (Hadfield, 2018, p. 26) in the language classroom.

Teachers obviously cannot be responsible for everything that students take away from learning activities, but these examples do indicate that we need to be aware of messages that we might be conveying to our students as we enact the curriculum with them in our classrooms. Probably one of the best ways to try to avoid problematic situations is to plan carefully.

222

From Application to Implementation

> **Further Reading**
>
> Edwards, R. (2015). Software and the hidden curriculum in digital education. *Pedagogy, Culture and Society*, *23*, 265–279.
>
> *Sample Study*
>
> Wette, R. (2010). Product-process distinctions in ELT curriculum theory and practice. *English Language Teaching Journal*, *65*(2), 136–144.

D. Planning Activities

Nero (2005) suggests a number of strategies that teachers should bear in mind when planning activities, one of which we highlight here because it is so important for identity work in classrooms: getting to know your students. If we wish to meet our students' needs, we have to get to know them well. Graves (2001, p. 179) suggests a number of aspects that we should attempt to understand. Probably the most straightforward is to develop some kind of insight into their English proficiency level. The following questions might be useful:

- Are they able to take part in simple conversations?
- To what extent can they read and write the language?
- Do they have a so-called spiky profile in that they have strengths in certain areas but are very weak in others?

It is also important to know about students' motivation:

- Why are they studying English?
- Are they in the class because they have to be there?
- Do they have personal needs or desires to learn the language?
- Is their attitude toward English positive?

These questions are important. The global reach of English is universally accepted. It is the language of business, politics, and increasingly tertiary education (Koo, 2009). The importance of learning English is accepted by countries around the world, who view mastery of the language as

223

From Application to Implementation

essential for career success. These conditions promote significant motivation for students and lead to their investment in further learning, and consequently (as Norton, 2013, has shown), investment in their identities. In other words, learning English changes who they are.

However, there is also widespread concern that the promotion of English comes at a cost. In the Arabic-speaking world, for example, there are concerns that the growing importance of English might lead to Western ways being more highly valued than Arab culture and customs. In particular, it is feared that this embracing of English might weaken religious belief because Arabic is the language of the Quran (Al-Qahtani & Al-Zumor, 2016). The Arab world is worried that this might lead to the erosion of Arab identity. Other ethnic groups around the world possibly share these misgivings.

It is entirely possible, therefore, that our learners might have mixed feelings about learning English. On the one hand, they value the opportunities a knowledge of English can provide, but on the other, they might not be happy with its dominance.

It would be difficult to overestimate the importance of students' cultural backgrounds, and the role culture plays in student identity. Kramsch (1993) says simply that culture is "the underlying dimension for what one knows and does" (p. 186). It is therefore essential that part of knowing your students is knowing their cultural backgrounds and practices, and consequently, making your teaching culturally responsive. In the classroom, teachers need to ensure that different cultures are acknowledged and respected, and they need to encourage understanding and empathy for different ways of living and thinking (Gay, 2000).

For all the activities in Part 2, we have tried to adopt a culturally responsive approach. For example, *Activity 19: Idiomatic Language* examines idiomatic expressions in the students' own languages. It emphasizes a rich variety of images and meanings and uses this variety as a background for the exploration of idiomatic English. Gay notes too that culturally responsive classrooms also need to be places where the transformative nature of education is acknowledged, where we

224

From Application to Implementation

can support our students to become people who make considered decisions and are prepared to act on these decisions in their personal, social and political lives. This integrity will be an important part of who they are and who they become.

There are numerous activities in the book that invite students to think about social issues in relation to their own lives and cultural communities. For example, we canvass attitudes toward gay men, examine issues to do with sustainable farming, and question social issues made explicit in advertising. We speculate on the environmental impact of various means of transport, and we problematize identity issues on Facebook. We have tried to select issues that we believe are pertinent to language learners' lives and the shaping of their identities in the modern world.

In this section, we have raised a number of broad issues worth keeping in mind as you go about planning for the implementation of the activities in your classroom. In Section E, we turn to the consideration of more specific suggestions for how you can bring these activities to life in your own classrooms in ways that are both enjoyable and effective.

E. Implementing Activities in the Classroom

In this section, we focus more specifically on the selection and implementation of the activities in Part 2, and suggest ways in which you can adapt them to suit your own particular circumstances. To do this, we ask you to consider answers to a set of six questions:

Question 1: Which of these identity-related activities do I think will appeal to my students? Why?

Question 2: Which of these activities best allow me to teach the language that I believe my students need?

Question 3: Which of these activities can I use as they are presented in the book? Which ones need to be adapted or changed? Are there major difficulties that I face if I wish to teach some of these activities? What can I do to overcome these challenges?

225

From Application to Implementation

Question 4: What material do I need in order to teach these activities? Will I be able to access this material easily? Can I make it myself? If not, what can I substitute for the suggested materials?

Question 5: A number of these activities can be linked to other activities, although all except one (*Activity 34: Writing a Report*) can be taught as stand-alone activities. Do I want to link the activities? If so, how should I go about linking, ordering, and spacing these activities?

Question 6: Some of the activities have been planned so that they can involve other classes and teachers. Do I believe that this is a good idea? If I do, how would I put these activities into practice? If it is not possible or desirable for me to work with other classes, how can I adapt the activities so that they will work just for my students?

Because you know your students best, you will be in a position to judge which activities will likely have the most appeal. In what follows, we work through each of the six questions and, drawing on the activities in Part 2, present one or two examples to illustrate ways that you might want to use your answers as a basis for conducting the activities.

Question 1: Which of These Identity-Related Activities Do I Think Will Appeal to My Students? Why?

Activities that allow students to explore aspects of their own identities (*Reflexing Identity*) will probably be of interest. We are all interested in ourselves! There are a number of activities that fall very strongly into this category, such as *Activity 3: What Makes Me Me?*, in which students have to weigh up features of their own lives and decide which they think have most significance for them. *Activity 1: This Is (Not) Like Me* asks students to work through their course book and select a number of images. They then explain why these images do or do not reflect their interests. *Activity 37: What Kind of Wild*

226

Animal? is designed to be an entertaining way for students to select their favorite wild animal and then justify their selection. In other activities, students discover whether color preferences are linked to personality traits, how names (given names, nicknames, or pet names) are linked to feelings of identity, they talk about how clothes reflect who we are, and they also explore what we find or don't find funny and why.

However, because students are not only interested in themselves, there are activities that ask them to consider environmental concerns and social justice issues. They get the opportunity to consider how their attitudes and opinions have an impact on who they are and how they fit into their world (e.g., issues to do with sexuality, advertising, and sourcing food). We have included activities that encourage learners to think critically and objectively in ways we believe they will find interesting (e.g., *Activity 7: Using Our Brains!*, *Activity 11: Chickens in Cages*, and *Activity 46: Social Justice and Advertising*). We have designed these activities to appeal to students and we have set many of our activities in the 21st century to ensure their relevance. In particular, activities such as *Activity 4: Tweeting*, *Activity 18: Why Is Facebook so Popular?*, and *Activity 40: Names for Online Gamers* address student interest in identities in the online environment.

Question 2: Which of These Activities Best Allow Me to Teach the Language That I Believe My Students Need?

Each activity has a box which identifies the particular language skills that are being addressed in the activity. In *Activity 20: Make Your Own Cartoon*, for example, the language focus is primarily on writing, particularly the use of direct and indirect speech. Is this appropriate language activity for your learners? Is this what they need at their stage of language development? Is the related identity content in the activity appropriate for their level of language proficiency?

From Application to Implementation

Language practice	
Skills?	listening, speaking, writing, visual literary
What?	using direct speech to tell a story or joke, using indirect speech to tell a story or joke, writing dialogue in a cartoon, writing indirect speech
How?	working individually to draw cartoons using speech bubbles, using others' cartoons to practice writing indirect speech

As another example, *Activity 6: Maps of the World* illustrates how specific vocabulary can be taught. You could make use of this activity to design your own activities, focusing on the specific vocabulary you wish to teach—vocabulary that is appropriate to the proficiency level and interest of your students.

A number of the activities focus on the use of conjunctions (e.g., *Activity 14: What's in a Name?*), but others look at the language students need to put their own points of view across, and justify their arguments (e.g., *Activity 11: Chickens in Cages*, *Activity 23: Justifying Your Opinion*, and *Activity 48: Transport of the Future*). The wide range of language areas and skills covered in the 48 activities means that there is a lot to choose from (and adapt if necessary), but it is important to remember that identity, *communicating identities*, is the primary focus of all the activities and the rationale for the way the activities have been organized in Part 2.

Question 3: Which of These Activities Can I Use as They Are Presented in the Book? Which Ones Need To Be Adapted or Changed? Are There Major Difficulties That I Face If I Wish to Teach Some of These Activities? What Can I Do to Overcome These Challenges?

You will be able to use many of the activities just as they are presented in Part 2. The time allocation, materials, and procedures will be appropriate to your teaching setting. However, it is quite likely that in some

228

From Application to Implementation

instances, there will be factors that make it difficult to use the activities without making some changes.

One of these factors has to do with *class size*. The activities have been designed with a class size of approximately 20 to 25 students in mind. However, you might be teaching a far larger or smaller class. Obviously, this will have an impact on group activities. When the class is small, an easy solution in some cases will be to have the students work in pairs instead of groups and then come together as a class to discuss the activities. An activity such as *Activity 44: Different Perspectives* falls into this category. In other activities the group approach is essential. If the class is very small, you might want to consider using the whole class as a group. Examples of these lessons are *Activity 46: Social Justice and Advertising* and *Activity 36: The Language of Ads*.

However, this will not work for all group activities. For example, in *Activity 7: Using Our Brains!*, a small class size will present challenges. The activity calls for small groups of three or four students to discuss the good, bad, and interesting points of a proposition. These small groups then join other groups discussing the same aspect. You could decide that you will only have one round of discussion, that is, there will simply be three groups examining the good, the bad, and the interesting. You might believe, though, that students will gain by exploring the points they have raised for a second time with fresh insights. If this is the case, you could ask the students to work individually and then share insights in groups.

If you have a large class, you might well be concerned that some students will take advantage of the group size and engage minimally in the required task. Perhaps more worrying is the possibility that others will be marginalized because of their relatively lower English proficiency level. This could be a real concern in an activity such as *Activity 35: No Laughing Matter* in which students are asked to write a report collaboratively. One possibility would be to limit the size of groups even if that means having as many as 10 or 11 groups in the classroom. This might be a better way to ensure that students are involved in the group activity, but the downside would be a heavy marking load. You might well decide to

From Application to Implementation

persist with bigger groups despite these challenges. Large groups have the advantage of offering a variety of different insights and opinions, and often students learn a great deal from other group members.

A further difficulty that you might face is that of *timing*. Some of the activities might not suit the timetabling schedule of your institution, or some students might work faster or slower than the envisaged guidelines. If the time available for teaching is more than that allocated for the activity you might want to link two activities together. There are a number of activities that have been designed to be taught in tandem (see later in this section). You might also want to extend the scope of the activities by consulting the recommendations in the *Extension* section added to many of the activities.

If your lesson time allocations are shorter than the time indicated in the activities, you might want to reduce the scope of the activity. In *Activity 5: Memories and Smells*, for example, you could skip the first section, which asks students to identify a number of smells, and instead provide a list of these to the students and then proceed with the rest of the activity. Alternatively, you could use two lesson periods to complete the activity.

One of the more difficult challenges you might face is a lack of *internet access* in the classroom. A few of the activities assume that this is available in the classroom or that your students have mobile or smart phones. An example of this is *Activity 32: Questioning National Identities*. In this activity, students are asked to determine the characteristics of people from different countries using an online search. If your students do not have access to the internet in the classroom or the school, it might be possible for you to print out articles from online sources, such as Wikipedia, yourself. Copies of these articles could then be made available to groups of students. This would enable them to complete the activity successfully, although the opportunity to develop the research skills necessary to find the information online would be lost. You could also use as a source information the work your students produce in *Activity 31: Stereotyping*. In this activity, students examine cultural identity traits associated with particular nationalities. Their own work therefore could serve as a very useful source of information for

230

From Application to Implementation

the *Questioning National Identity* activity and have the added bonus of showing students how their own work can be shared with others. This can be very empowering.

Lack of internet access can be overcome quite easily in other ways, too. *Activity 4: Tweeting* is an activity that attempts to develop students' ability to identify what is important in a text and to summarize this information succinctly. To do so, the activity requires students to adopt the Twitter convention of using only 140 characters. While this activity asks students to find a news item online, this is not the only way to approach the activity. You could photocopy a number of newspaper articles and allow students to use these instead for the activity, for example.

For all activities, it is important to read through them fully before deciding to make any adjustments. Regarding the use of the internet, for example, some activities, despite their name do not require any internet access at all; e.g., *Activity 18: Why Is Facebook So Popular?* and *Activity 40: Names for (Online) Gamers*.

Question 4: What Material Do I Need to Teach These Activities? Will I Be Able to Access This Material Easily? Can I Make It Myself? If Not, What Can I Substitute for the Suggested Materials?

Many of the activities require nothing more than typical classroom equipment—a whiteboard (or a blackboard) and paper and writing utensils for students. There are some though that do require more materials. Later, we again suggest illustrative answers to this question related to some of the activities in Part 2.

In activities such as *Activity 3: What Makes Me Me?* and *Activity 45: What Makes Them Them?* you are asked to provide students with magazine pictures. If you do not have access to these pictures, colleagues may be willing to help you with this, or you could ask students to bring magazines to class. Students may also prefer to express themselves with their own drawings or paintings, or they could even investigate other ways of presenting their identities, such as through performance—singing a song,

231

From Application to Implementation

telling a story, acting out an incident. This, too, could be done individually or in groups. If it is possible, you might want to make a recording of the performance so that this could be kept as a record, and then potentially used for further activities.

Activity 6: Maps of the World requires a traditional map showing Greenland at the top and another map with an alternative view, showing another country at the top. If you have difficulties sourcing such a map you could draw one yourself, or, as part of a preparatory activity, get your students in groups to draw a world map with a country of their choice at the top.

As a further example, if you are having difficulty finding texts for *Activity 29: Teacher Roles*, you might be able to persuade your teacher colleagues to write half a page about what they think a language teacher's role is. You could ensure that any identifying information is removed from the text. It could turn out to be a very interesting exercise if colleagues teaching in different environments were willing to participate.

Question 5: A Number of These Activities Can Be Linked to Other Activities, Although All Except One (*Activity 34: Writing a Report*) Can Be Taught as Stand-Alone Activities. Do I Want to Link the Activities? If So, How Should I Go About Linking, Ordering, and Spacing These Activities?

While all activities can be used on their own, some are fairly loosely linked to others, and others are more closely associated with each other. *Activity 11: Chickens in Cages* and *Activity 23: Justifying Your Opinion* are two examples that are quite closely linked. In the first activity, students read a text about the farming of poultry. As well as asking students to consider differences between formal and informal writing, the activity requires them to consider the advantages and disadvantages of keeping hens in cages. The students note their responses on a worksheet. *Justifying Your Opinion* builds on the work of the first activity as far as formal or informal language is concerned and asks students to

232

From Application to Implementation

use the identified advantages and disadvantages to serve as the basis for a short written opinion piece.

One of the advantages of these closely linked activities is that students are able to make use of their own work in subsequent activities and thus build on their own material. If classes are long (i.e., close to two hours), these linked activities could work very well. However, there is also the possibility that students will grow tired of caged hens and color choices! If linked activities are taught separately, it is probably wise not to allow too much time between the activities, or you might have to spend quite a bit of class time reminding students about what was done in the first activity.

The linking of activities is something to bear in mind when you are planning a unit of work that covers a term or a semester. In such a case, you might want to ensure that any material used or generated in an earlier activity is safely stored for use in the later related activity.

Question 6: Some of the Activities Have Been Planned So That They Can Involve Other Classes and Teachers. Do I Believe That This Is a Good Idea? If I Do, How Would I Put These Activities Into Practice? If It Is Not Possible or Desirable for Me to Work With Other Classes, How Can I Adapt the Activities So That They Will Work Just for My Students?

Activity 3: What Makes Me Me? requires students to make a collage to depict who they are. As an alternative, students can perform their identities. If your students are happy to do so, their collages could be displayed on the classroom walls, and teachers and students from other classes could be invited to come and look at them. Your students might be given an opportunity to explain their art, and the visiting students could ask them questions. If your students have opted for a performance, students from other classes could act as the audience and again be encouraged to ask questions about the significance of what they have observed. Your fellow teachers could use the opportunity to ask their classes to decide which of the collages they liked best and why.

From Application to Implementation

They could write this up as a short report or have a class discussion. For this particular activity, it is not necessary for other teachers and classes to be involved—whether this is a good idea or not will be your decision. We have merely shown here how it might be possible.

However, two activities that might more obviously benefit from being done in collaboration with other classes are *Activity 33: Designing a Questionnaire* and *Activity 34: Writing a Report*. In the first activity, students design a questionnaire that aims to test if certain colors are linked to personality traits. This questionnaire is then administered to another class, and their responses (identified only by a number) are analyzed and written up as a report by the students who developed the questionnaire. The completed reports can be returned to the participants if they were interested. It is also quite possible to use these two activities in the same class. The class could be split in half with each half developing its own questionnaire to be answered by the other half. You would be in the best position to decide which of these options would be most effective for your students.

F. What Should We Do After the Activities?

Graves (2008) refers to *curriculum enactment* as educational experiences that are created by students and teachers working together in the classroom. What is important is that classrooms should be places "where knowledge and practice are distributed among participants so that each participant has something to contribute and something to learn" (p. 167). Of course, not all lessons are successful. A teacher might find that students are not particularly interested in what she or he has prepared, or they don't appear to have learned what was taught to them. This happens to all of us at times, even when we have taken a great deal of time and trouble with our preparation.

While a 'failed' lesson can be very discouraging, we can gain valuable insights if we are prepared to unpack what went wrong. Often, we can learn more from a lesson that didn't succeed than one that did. While we are teaching, we are aware that the lesson is not going to plan— as teachers, we are always thinking on our feet—but we cannot stop the lesson to examine the issues more deeply at that specific point in

234

From Application to Implementation

time. What we need to do after class is to reflect on what happened and gather evidence from the lesson. We might note for instance that a particular activity went well up to a point and then the students appeared to lose interest. We would then be able to examine what happened at that point and reflect on what we could have been done differently. We might realize that the work we asked them to do was too difficult or too easy or possibly that they didn't see its relevance.

Reflection allows us to make changes that improve our practice. You will have noticed that each activity ends with a section encouraging teacher reflection. The aim of the reflection is to encourage you to think about the activity as far as your own practice is concerned. That is why in Part 4 of this book we address the concept of reflection more systematically in terms of exploratory action research. We explain this approach and suggest how teachers can explore their own practice systematically, use the insights gained to plan better and more effective activities in the short term, and develop professionally in the longer term.

In Part 1 of this book, we pointed out that the aim of the activities in Part 2 is to provide learners with an opportunity to reflect on the various facets of identity, both individually and in groups. We realize that these processes are influenced by what actually happens as the teacher and the learners enact the curriculum in the classroom. However, it is important that we emphasize that no activity alone and no accompanying advice, no matter how well constructed, can ever come anywhere close to matching the importance of the teacher, and in particular the impact a *creative* teacher can have on learners.

Further Reading

Jones, R. H., & Richards, J. C. (Eds.). (2016). *Creativity in language teaching: Perspectives from research and practice*. New York, NY: Routledge.

Sample Study

Tin, T. N. (2013). Towards creativity in ELT: The need to say something new. *English Language Teaching Journal, 67*(4), 385–397.

From Application to Implementation

We had this idea of *creativity* very much in mind when we designed the activities. We hope that what we have produced will spark learner creativity, but perhaps just as important, that it will spark yours. Research tells us that student creativity can be enhanced through social modeling and the classroom environment (Soh, 2017). Social modelling in an educational setting refers to the way that students imitate the behavior of teachers. If teachers practice creativity in the classroom, students are likely to follow their example. And if teachers foster an environment in which students feel safe, they will follow their own creative urges and try out new ideas. We would therefore like to encourage you to be creative with the activities—to take ownership of them—by using them as they are or turning them into something that is useful, interesting, and exciting for you and your students.

Part 4

From Implementation to Research

A. Introduction

In Part 1, we discussed research-informed conceptualizations of language learner and teacher identity. The research focuses on the experiences of learners and teachers in their classrooms and schools and also more broadly in the sociocultural contexts that interconnect with the experiences. These broader contexts may seem far removed from the daily reality of classroom action, but the recent research issues and developments that De Costa and Norton (2016) outline, such as those related to globalization and digital literacy, for example, show that what happens in the world outside of classrooms affects what happens inside them, and this includes the shaping of the identities of the people in those spaces.

The implications of the identity research described in Part 1 informed the practice-oriented activities in Part 2 and the suggestions for their implementation in curricula in Part 3. Part 4 presents the final stage in the research-practice-research cycle. In this stage, the classroom practitioner becomes the researcher. Some reasons for conducting further explorations of your professional practices relate to self-reflection or functioning as a reflective practitioner (Farrell, 2015), with the aim of improving teaching and learning. Other reasons relate to problems or worrying puzzles in the classroom, with the aim of addressing these challenges.

Identity is the focus of exploration in Part 4. The aim is for teacher explorers to promote and retain identity issues—both their learners' and their own—on their teaching and learning agenda. The type of research we advocate is *exploratory action research*, a form of practitioner research that aims not to "place too much of an extra burden on you as a busy teacher" (Smith & Rebolledo, 2018).

237

From Implementation to Research

Exploratory action research achieves this by incorporating all research processes as much as possible into regular classroom teaching and learning activities.

We also advocate for the use of stories during the exploratory research. Stories told and shared by learners and teachers are all around us. We tell stories all the time. In telling the stories, we make meaning of our experiences—in other words, we understand them better, and so do those that we share them with. It makes sense, therefore, to use those stories for research purposes. Stories are central to a research approach called *narrative inquiry*, an approach that has a long history of use *by* teachers *for* teachers (see Johnson & Golombek, 2002). We suggest ways in which narrative methods can be integrated with the steps of exploratory action research.

B. Organization of Part 4

Part 4 begins by briefly outlining the principles and goals of exploratory action research and then describes the steps to follow when actually conducting research in your classroom. In Section D, we suggest strategies for selecting topics to explore, including drawing on the activities and teacher reflections in Part 2. We then present ways to conduct exploratory action research, including collecting information or data (Section E), analyzing or making sense of the data (Section G), and then reporting the findings (Section H). Section F suggests ways in which stories can be incorporated into the processes of exploratory action research.

C. What Is Exploratory Action Research?

Exploratory action research involves both *exploration* and *action*; it is exploratory research followed by action research. Smith and Rebolledo (2018, p. 26) associate a question with each of these stages:

Exploration:	What is the current situation?
Action:	What are the effects of the change(s) that I attempt?

From Implementation to Research

Answering the first question involves three steps (see Smith & Rebolledo, 2018):

A. *Planning to explore*: At this stage, you decide what your topic will be (see Section D later) and what questions you will ask about that topic; in other words, what do you plan to explore? Other planning involves how you will collect your data—the information will help you answer your questions—and how you will go about systematically analyzing that data. The analyzing is still some way off, but it is good to plan in advance to ensure you have the necessary resources available, including time and skills.

B. *Exploring*: This is the observing, listening, recording, or surveying you do to collect the data necessary to answer your questions and puzzles. As we'll see later (Section E), with exploratory action research, the aim is to try to embed these data-gathering activities into your usual classroom practice as much as possible so as not to add extra workload to your already busy everyday teaching life.

C. *Analyzing and interpreting*: At this stage, you examine the information you have collected. In the process, you interpret what you find (see Section G), based obviously on the data but also drawing on your own experience as a professional educator and on your familiarity with the situation in which the exploration is conducted. Analysis and interpretation lead to a better understanding of your research topic, and more specifically, answers to your research questions.

Smith and Rebolledo (2018) point out that "these three steps may be enough—the new understanding you gain can help, in many ways, on its own" (p. 26). The exploratory research phase, in other words, may have served the purpose of helping you solve a puzzle, confirm your views about an issue, or understand a situation that interested you.

However, if there is a need or desire to continue onto action, the second question comes into play: What are the effects of the

From Implementation to Research

change(s) I attempt? Smith and Rebolledo (2018), in line with the principles and processes of exploratory action research, suggest the following four steps:

1. *Plan*: Action research is about intervention—to act in order to bring about a change to your practice (see strategies for selecting topics in Section D later). So, at this stage of the exploratory action research trajectory, the planning involves deciding what needs to be changed and how to collect further information (data) to monitor the effects of the change. Again, it is a good idea to plan your approach to analysis to ensure you have the resources (including time and research skills) available.
2. *Act*: Here, you act! The intervention is applied. For example, if the problem to be explored (the topic) is ineffective group work and you have a plan for an intervention that involves adjusting the number of students in a group, then the action (or intervention) is assigning group work with the newly adjusted number of students.
3. *Observe*: You then need to see what happens as a result of the action. This involves collecting data, either while the planned action is being performed (e.g., recording classroom talk) or afterward (e.g., making notes), as well as analyzing the data collected.
4. *Reflect*: Finally, at this very important stage, you reflect on what happened and try to make sense of it all. In other words, the aim here is to determine the effects of the action: Has it answered your research question? Has the outcome of the action helped you solve your problem or your puzzle? Do you feel satisfied that you have a better understanding of the issue you set out to explore?

Also important at the *Reflect* stage is to decide whether further exploration (starting at A) or action research (starting at 1) is needed. In addition, towards the end of your exploratory action research you may want to consider sharing your research findings (see Section H later). Figure 4.1 shows the steps involved in the whole process.

From Implementation to Research

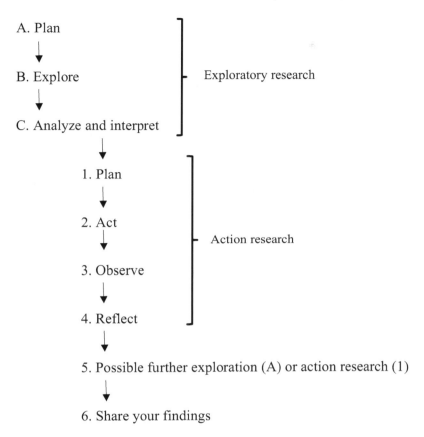

Figure 4.1 Steps in exploratory action research

> ### Further Reading
>
> Dikilitaş, K., & Hanks, J. (Eds.). (2018). *Developing language teachers with exploratory practice*. Cham, Switzerland: Palgrave Macmillan.
>
> ### *Sample Study*
>
> Wyatt, M., & Márquez, C. P. (2016). Helping first-year undergraduates engage in language research. *Language Teaching Research*, 20(2), 146–164.

From Implementation to Research

D. Selecting Topics to Explore

When choosing a topic to explore, it is important to remember that exploratory action research aims to blend the research processes into regular classroom practice as much as possible, so as not to place too much burden on you as a busy teacher. This applies both to ways of researching (i.e., the methods you use to collect and analyze data) and to the *topics* you choose to focus on. In other words, the topics should emerge from your own teaching and your own experiences in your institutions and broader educational environments. Below are five recommendations to help you select topics for your exploratory research, as well as to keep you focused on identity.

1. Reflection on Classroom Life

The most obvious and efficient way to generate identity-related topics for exploratory action research is to reflect on life in your own classroom and school context. This means reflecting on the teaching and learning that all classroom participants—the characters that make up the world of the classroom—engage in as they interact together. Reflecting with a colleague is also a good way to articulate some of your thoughts and ideas. The following broad categories can help focus your reflection.

- *You, the teacher*: your emotions, your sense of efficacy, your needs and desires, your stresses and achievements, your goals and ambitions for the future
- *Your learners*: their level of motivation, their attitudes, their (lack of) participation, their discipline, identity categories (e.g., race, age, nationality, religion, culture)
- *Teaching*: acknowledging diversity, appropriate teaching approaches, equitable assessment methods
- *Materials and technology*: selecting appropriate materials, making technology available, teaching and maintaining online communication etiquette
- *Language skills*: the teaching and learning of listening, speaking, reading, writing

242

From Implementation to Research

- *Language systems*: the teaching and learning of grammar, vocabulary, phonology, discourse
- *Classroom management*: class size issues, assigning learners to groups, handling behavioral problems

2. Manageable, Urgent, Significant, and Engaging (MUSE)

Reflecting on classroom life may generate a number of potential topics but leave you unsure about which of these to choose. Smith and Rebolledo (2018, p. 31) suggest a useful way to classify these topics in order to narrow down your focus.

- *Manageable*: Is the topic you wish to explore one that is possible with the resources currently available to you? Resources include your time, equipment, information, and other people (e.g., participants and any assistants or collaborators). You might have a good idea for a topic but find that the necessary resources are not available. For example, observing learner participation in small group interaction might be a worthy project, but lack of audio- or video-recording equipment could limit the amount or value of the data collected.
- *Urgent*: Are there issues or problems that need to be addressed through exploratory research as soon as possible? Urgent issues might include those that relate to (a) health and safety, (b) emotional well-being—your learners' and your own, and (c) serious assessment or pedagogical matters. An example might be the need to collect evidence for a proposal you wish to submit to your manager to review the school's placement policy since you have noticed that some learners are disadvantaged by being placed at an inappropriate level on entry to the school.
- *Significant*: What research topics are significant in that they will benefit you and your teaching, your learners, or your school and community? These topics are not urgent in that they need to be addressed as soon as possible, but they are important because the benefits will be measurable and possibly bring about positive change. Typical examples in this category include asking questions about your learners' lack of motivation and examining the

243

From Implementation to Research

outcomes of trying an innovative pair-work activity or reducing the number of time-consuming assessments over the course of a semester.

- *Engaging*: Is the topic something you are really interested in and even passionate about? If it is then you are more likely to engage fully in the research and feel that you are not wasting your time on the project. Engaging topics are those that emerge from your own context—that apply to your teaching situation—rather than those that are suggested by others. They offer questions or puzzles you really want to find answers to. You will feel excited about planning and starting the project, and you will actually enjoy conducting the exploration and sharing the outcomes with others.

3. Activities in Part 2

The 48 activities in Part 2 provide a rich source of topics. To begin with, the activities are grouped together into the four major identity facets—*reflexing, projecting, recognizing, and imagining*—and so four broad identity-related topic areas are already suggested. Each activity then deals with some aspects of identity to focus your thinking, including identity categories (e.g., gender, ethnicity, age) and the way identities are communicated in interaction. Learner contributions to the activities will also produce huge amounts of information that may suggest further avenues for exploration. So listen carefully to what they say, observe what they do, and take notes. The following are examples of potential research topics arising from two activities.

- *Activity 25: A Good Friend (Recognizing Identity)*: In this activity, your students identify characteristics of a good friend (reflecting silently and independently), share them with each other (in pairs, by walking around the classroom, and in whole-class discussion), and generate lists of vocabulary and phrases that describe friendship. It is an elementary level activity. Do this lesson plan and the content it covers suggest any possible identity-related research topics?

From Implementation to Research

a. How interested were the students in exploring the theme of 'friendship'? Could this be a theme worth developing further in your course? How?

b. Did related (more interesting) themes emerged from the activity? Is 'interest' a concept worth exploring in your class?

c. Was the activity too easy or too difficult? How about measuring learners' perceptions of 'difficulty level' as a research topic?

- *Activity 8: The Genders of Objects (Reflexing Identity)*: This activity has students considering the grammatical gender of objects and how this relates to perceptions of conventional human gender identities. It also asks students to reflect on their own gendered identities. There is opportunity for discussion and debate. Does this activity have the capacity to spark a research idea?

  a. What is the gender mix of the class? Did this have an effect on the way the activity unfolded, and how could the activity be done differently with classes of different gender mixes?

  b. Is gender a topic students want to explore more? Why? And how does gender intersect with their interest in other identity categories, such as sexuality and religion?

  c. Could you ask the students to suggest a related research topic for you?

4. Post-Activity Teacher Reflections in Part 2

Each activity ends with a Teacher Reflection. The aim of the reflections is to give you the opportunity to think about the activity—its content, its aims, its effectiveness in getting your learners to communicate their identities—in terms of your own practice and identity as a language teacher. How does what the activity is about relate to your professional life as a teacher? Does the activity spark a thought or memory or emotion that resonates with who you are as a teacher? Has the activity any connection to how you see yourself as a teacher in the future?

245

From Implementation to Research

In doing the reflections, therefore, you have already made a good start in your search for a research topic. The reflection process should generate ideas that can be molded into a more concrete topic for further exploration. The four identity facets—*reflexing, projecting, recognizing, imagining*—into which the teacher reflections are categorized provide additional guidance for identifying a topic. Consider the following two examples.

- *Activity 31: Stereotyping (Recognizing Identity)*: This activity requires students to examine their own cultural or national identities and those of their fellow students and to then compare and contrast any stereotypes that might become evident. The activity entails sharing of opinions and class discussion. In the Teacher Reflection, you are asked to consider your own stereotypes and how they might affect your relationships with your learners and your teaching practice. Is there a potential research topic here?

    a. Is there something worth exploring that might develop your understanding of cultural diversity?
    b. How could this new knowledge be applied to equitable class-room practice (e.g., assigning learners into groups or pairs, calling on students to answer questions, grading assessments)?
    c. Is there potential for changing in some small way who you are—your identity—as a teacher?

- *Activity 42: Speaking English Tomorrow (Imagining Identity)*: In this activity, learners imagine a future social encounter during which they will use English. They complete a narrative frame that describes the outcome of the encounter including how it makes them feel. The Teacher Reflection asks you to do the same thing and then to transfer the imagined experience to your classroom life. Does this reflection prompt any research topics?

    a. Does imagining future language activity offer any research topics that can be useful for classroom teaching and learning?
    b. How does imagining future language use and learning affect your students' motivation to learn?

246

From Implementation to Research

c. Is there a relationship between emotions and your imagined future teacher identity?

5. Further Topic Resources

In Barkhuizen's (2019) edited book on qualitative research topics in language teacher education, all contributing authors suggest strategies that researchers could use when selecting appropriate topics for their research. The researchers they had in mind were not necessarily teachers and their research approaches included others besides exploratory action research (and their topics were not only those related to identity). Their suggestions, however, do complement and extend those we have presented so far. Barkhuizen synthesized the authors' suggestions, and relevant ones are listed below. As you will see, some require personal reflection, others require work beyond the classroom, and others align quite closely with the practices of exploratory action research (i.e., being integrated into ongoing classroom practice).

a. Read theoretical and empirical literature.

- Be attentive to current debates and developments.
- Read content pages and abstracts of recent, relevant journals and newsletters.

b. Follow interests and passions.

- Be constantly engaged in critical self-reflection of your own experience.
- Ground topics in context you know and care about.
- Connect topic to your own life history, including language learning history.

c. Engage with professional and academic community.

- Join professional associations and read their research agendas and missions.
- Attend workshops and conferences and be a critical listener.
- Participate in online forums, discussion groups, and webinars.

247

From Implementation to Research

d. Engage with teachers.

- Observe teachers in classrooms.
- Observe your own workplace.
- Consider what issues face teachers and learners in their contexts from their perspectives.

e. Be curious.

- Pay attention to debates and discussions in the media.
- Reflect on your own professional problems and issues and reasons for them.
- Pursue questions you really don't have answers to and are really curious about.

f. Explore your own workplace.

- Talk to colleagues.
- Consider collaborating in research teams.
- Draw on professional knowledge and teaching practice in your own teaching.

g. Be practical.

- Ensure you have access to relevant participants.
- Consider whether you have the necessary research skills needed to conduct the research.
- Consider whether there are sufficient resources (i.e., human, financial, time, bibliographic) needed to conduct the research.

h. Be prepared for the unexpected.

- Be on the lookout for topics that emerge when busily research-ing or working on something else.
- Take notice of discomfort, ambiguities, and puzzlement in your work, from which topics might emerge.

E. Gathering Information

Data collection or information gathering takes place at two stages along the exploratory action research journey: during the initial

248

From Implementation to Research

exploration and then again to observe the effect of the action or intervention. Smith and Rebolledo (2018) describe 12 data collection methods, or "sources of information" (p. 42). These are common among teacher researchers (see Borg, 2013), particularly those employing methods associated with exploratory practice or action research when the goal is to embed the research activities as much as possible into regular classroom practice.

We start by simply listing seven of the methods with a brief explanation of each and then provide more concrete suggestions for the remaining five because they are potentially more useful for investigating identity-related topics. The latter create opportunities, through speaking or writing, for reflecting on and sharing life experiences from the perspective of the person doing the sharing, whether it is you, other teachers, or your learners, thus being suitable for identity research.

However, creative use of the first seven methods might also produce relevant information about an identity topic you have chosen to investigate. For example, depending on how you design a questionnaire—the questions you ask and the way responses are recorded—might reveal a lot about some aspect of the respondent's identity.

1. *Other people's written ideas on the topic*: reading what other people have written about your topic (may require visiting the library or surfing the web) and how this relates to your ideas
2. *Responses to a questionnaire*: designing a survey questionnaire and distributing to your students, or other teachers or administrators, depending on what your research focus is
3. *Lesson plans and materials*: examining your choices and use, and the students' reception of the lessons you plan and how these play out in your classroom
4. *Lesson recordings*: recording and then listening to (or watching if you video record) classroom interaction or your own classroom talk
5. *A critical friend's notes about your lesson*: asking a friendly colleague to comment non-judgmentally on aspects of your teaching (from recordings or real-life classroom observations)

From Implementation to Research

6. *Pictures of your class*: taking pictures of classroom furniture arrangements, in which students sit or move for various activities and in which your own favorite positions are for moving and standing and storing materials and equipment (be aware privacy or ethical issues might arise if taking photos of students)
7. *Students' performance on tasks (written or recorded)*: observing and analyzing students' engagement in activities or assessments (written or oral) and their achievement

Your own written reflections or notes

- You write freely when time allows about your ideas and feelings during or after a lesson or unit of work.
- You write a blog, which you share with colleagues or online to a community of practice (and invite comments).
- You keep a regular journal in which you write about how things are going with your teaching, your professional development, a particular issue or concern, or your plans for the future.

Reflective writing by students

- Learners reflect on their experiences of classroom life in response to questions from you in the form of notes or paragraphs.
- Learners keep language learning diaries.
- Learners write a language learning history.
- Students write regular letters to you as a writing activity (a closed group Facebook page, if applicable, could be used for this).
- Learners' reflections could be multimodal, incorporating pictures, drawings, and photographs.

Notes or recordings of focus group discussions

- Small groups of learners or teachers get together face to face to discuss a topic that relates to your research topic.
- Teacher groups get together using Zoom or Skype.
- The discussion is audio recorded, for later careful listening and note taking, or transcribing if time allows.

250

From Implementation to Research

- You take notes during the discussion if you are part of the group.
- A closed WhatsApp or Facebook group of teachers continues the discussion.

Notes or recordings of interviews with individuals

- You interview a learner, a fellow teacher, a parent, or an administrator about *their* identity experiences.
- You interview the above for their perceptions on *your* practice and development.
- You prepare questions or topics that will invite conversation and storytelling, rather than yes-or-no answers.
- You take notes during the interview or afterward.
- Preferably, you audio record the interview, for repeated listening (and possible transcribing if time allows).

Notes from informal conversations with colleagues

- You talk informally with friendly colleagues about your daily teaching experiences, feelings, issues, and concerns.
- You make a regular meeting time (over coffee or lunch) to share professional stories—both real and imagined for the future.
- You keep notes, but don't let that distract from the conversation, so best to do so afterward.
- You talk by Skype or phone.
- You invite your colleague to contact you to have conversations focusing on *their* experiences, feelings, issues, and concerns (you can learn a lot about yourself in the process).

Although we have presented these methods separately, they can also be used in combination. Focus group discussion could be followed by individual interviews with selected members of the group, for example. A student's written reflection could be combined with what they say in a focus group or an interview. Your reflective journal writing might suggest topics to be explored further with your teacher conversational partner. Remember, though, not to be too ambitious because time is always a factor in the busy lives of teacher researchers.

251

From Implementation to Research

F. Narrative Inquiry

Narrative inquiry is a research approach that makes use of stories to understand the life experiences of the people sharing the stories, from their perspective. Stories are central to the research process. The underlying assumption of narrative inquiry is that by telling stories and listening to them (or writing and reading them), we better understand or make sense of the experiences that the stories are about. You can see then why sharing stories would be attractive to researchers, particularly those interested in exploring identity. By researchers, we mean narrators researching their own experiences or researchers investigating the experiences of others.

Although this brief statement about narrative inquiry may appear rather straightforward, doing narrative inquiry is in fact a rather complex endeavor, for a number of reasons, including (1) there are numerous, sometimes contradictory, definitions of what *narrative* and *story* actually mean; (2) there is a diverse range of methods associated with narrative inquiry; and (3) the value of story in research as a means for understanding experience is frequently questioned.

Nevertheless, we all tell stories all the time about our experiences. Teachers tell stories about what happens in their classrooms, the learners they encounter, the problems they suffer, and the successes they enjoy, and learners tell stories about their learning, their teachers, their life challenges, and their desires for the future. So why not make use of these ubiquitous stories to learn more about what we do and who we are?

For those interested in pursuing a narrative-like approach to exploratory action research, at both exploratory and action phases, it is important to remember that *story* is central to the process. Narrative inquiry has at its core two basic procedures: (1) collecting stories and then analyzing them and (2) constructing stories from data. The first of these involves searching for stories in the data (see methods of collecting data in Section E earlier) and then interpreting what the stories tell us about the identity of the narrator.

From Implementation to Research

(a) Collecting Stories ⟶ Analyzing Stories

Two questions in this process become relevant: (1) How do we recognize a story? And (2) How do we go about analyzing the story? There are different theoretical and cultural perspectives on what a story is, but generally we tend to know what a story 'looks like'. Some elements that might be familiar to you include the following:

- Stories narrate experiences from the past or the imagined future. They tell about something that happened or will happen in the life of the person telling the story.
- They include reflective commentary on those experiences— comments that portray emotions and beliefs associated with the experiences.
- They typically have a temporal or time-related dimension. In other words, something happens over a period of time, like a plot. There is some 'action' in the story.
- Stories always make reference, implicitly or explicitly, to *who* was involved in the story action (characters in the story world), *when* the action took place (time), and *where* it happened (place and space).
- Stories have relatively high *tellability*, which refers to the extent to which an account conveys a sequence of reportable events and makes a point in a rhetorically effective manner (novel, unusual, unique) (Ochs & Capps, 2001).

In analyzing stories (see more in Section G later), a good place to start is to focus on any information or themes that relate to the identity of the narrator, and one way to do this is to ask *who*, *when*, and *where* about them and then *why*, *how*, and *what* about the answers you get.

The second basic procedure involves constructing stories from the information that has been collected, which may or may not be in story form. This entails configuring the data into a coherent story form.

253

From Implementation to Research

(b) Collecting Data ⟶ Constructing Stories

This process is not as easy as it sounds. In writing the story, you are not merely summarizing the content of the data; you are also addressing your research topic. So, in effect, the writing of the narrative is actually *analysis* because you are interpreting the data at the same time as you are writing the story. The outcome is very effective. You will produce a readable account of the identity experiences of the narrator (yours or other people in your educational setting) that is informative and potentially useful for generating a deeper understanding of a particular practice or context or for bringing about change.

Further Reading

Barkhuizen, G., Benson, P., & Chik, A. (2014). *Narrative inquiry in language teaching and learning research*. New York, NY: Routledge.

Sample Study

Ford, K. (2016). The taped monologue as narrative technique for reflective practice. *English Language Teaching Journal, 70*(3), 253–260.

G. Making Sense of the Information Gathered

Analyzing data—interpreting it, understanding it, making sense of it—isn't always a neat, separate stage that follows data collection. Analysis really begins much earlier, even while the process of information gathering is taking place. For example, while conducting an interview, you are already beginning to make some interpretations about what you are hearing even though they might be tentative at that stage. If you decide to transcribe the interview, the process of transcribing is also analysis. Although your analysis may not yet be systematic, you begin to make interpretations about what you hear and write down along the way.

If you have taken any research methodology courses in your teacher training, you will be aware that there are many different approaches to data analysis. Traditionally, these approaches have been divided

254

From Implementation to Research

into two broad types: quantitative and qualitative. The former, as the name suggests, involves numbers—counting numbers and comparing numbers. Data that generates numbers include responses to closed-item (multiple choice) questionnaires and test scores, for example. You can immediately see that this sort of data and the accompanying analysis are not particularly suitable for researching *identity*, in which personal stories of experience, personal reflections, and emotions are foregrounded and interpreted. Qualitative analytical methods are more appropriate for exploring identities.

Qualitative analysis involves working with *text* rather than numbers. Text in its broadest sense refers to words—language—but also other semiotic resources such as drawings, pictures, photographs, signs, and gestures. These are ways in which we communicate with each other— ways we share our meanings and interpretations of life, including who we are (our identity) and how we see others.

There are various approaches to analyzing text data, ranging from more to less systematic. Some take more time (and effort) than others, and the outcomes (and value) of the analysis vary according to the approach taken. We suggest four ways for going about analyzing and interpreting your qualitative data, but it is important to note that these provide only a guideline and that you may discover methods more suitable to your own situation. Also, our suggestions can be combined to produce even more rigorous outcomes.

As a piece of illustrative data (Figure 4.2), we use the following extract from an interview with Alex, an English teacher and teacher educator who works at a public university in a large city in Colombia, South America. At the time of the interview, Alex was a PhD student, and in the interview, he explains why he decided to study further. Alex was a participant in a study that aimed to examine the reasons experienced in-service teachers and teacher educators had for continuing their professional development through formal study and how these reasons related to their transforming identity. As you will see, Alex's reasons for investing in further formal in-service study primarily have to do with advancing his knowledge of the subject area (curriculum design) he was teaching.

255

From Implementation to Research

1. well <u>I started to look for a PhD</u>[A] after three years working at the master's program
2. after three years six semesters six different groups of teachers
3. <u>I realized something</u>[B] there
4. and is that in my curriculum in <u>my module of curriculum design</u>[C]
5. the teachers <u>didn't have either epistemological instances</u>[D]
6. or <u>pedagogical instances</u>[D]
7. towards teaching or learning yeah
8. because the focus of <u>the module that I give isn't</u>[C] that yeah
9. what is curriculum
10. <u>but what is curriculum</u>[D] from an epistemological position
11. and pedagogical position
12. <u>well I realized that</u>[B]
13. and <u>I started to look for PhDs</u>[A]

Figure 4.2 Interview extract

Multiple Exposure and Critical Reflection

An effective way to explore your data is to become thoroughly familiar with it. That statement may sound obvious, but it is often ignored as good advice. Researchers can be too eager to get to the 'results' of their study and so dive into the mechanics of coding the data or doing a thematic analysis or some other technical procedure before actually knowing what the data is really about.

Exposure to the data means *looking at* it over and over again and in the process gaining a deeper understanding of what it is about. What *kind* of data (e.g., focus group discussion notes, language learner histories, your personal written reflections) and *how much* data (e.g., one teacher journal entry, multiple Facebook posts, 25 learner diaries) will determine the nature of your engagement with it. For example, a couple readings of one short teacher journal entry might be enough to get an idea of what it is about (and even if superficially, what is says about the identity of the teacher). But you might need to

From Implementation to Research

go back to a series of lengthy recorded conversations with a teacher colleague a number of times to recall and interpret the content.

It does not take too much exposure to the extract from Alex's interview to make some meaning from it (see Figure 4.2). We can tell quite easily that "after three years" (line 1) teaching pre-service English teachers in a master's program, Alex came to the realization ("I realized something there," line 3) that the content of his curriculum design course fell short of what he expected for his student teachers at their academic level. He thus perceived a 'gap' in an aspect of his teacher education practice. To address this situation, he "started to look for a PhD" (lines 1 and 13) that would provide him with the relevant knowledge to develop his course so that his students would begin to explore the construct of curriculum more deeply, beyond its mere theoretical definition. His concern appears to be how we learn or acquire knowledge from curriculum ("epistemological position," line 10) and how we apply the curriculum in teaching practice ("pedagogical position," line 11). Alex has invested in further graduate teacher education, therefore, not only to upskill himself and transform his language teacher educator identity in the process but ultimately to improve his course for the benefit his pre-service teachers.

The following are some strategies to keep in mind when 'looking at' the information you have gathered:

- Read the data over and over again.
- If audio recorded, listen to the data over and over again.
- Make notes of your (tentative) interpretations.
- Maintain your focus on your research topic.
- Talk to someone about your data and your interpretations and then go back to your data again.
- Continue to make notes and read them over and over again.
- Keep an open mind.
- View the data from multiple perspectives (e.g., teacher, learner, administrator, a younger you, a future you).
- If you are at the action research stage, start thinking about what to change.

From Implementation to Research

For some exploratory action research, *multiple exposure and critical reflection* may suffice as an approach to analysis. In other words, it may serve the purpose of learning enough about an issue or a puzzle (at the exploratory stage) or of observing the effect of an intervention (at the action stage). However, for other projects, further or a different kind of analysis might be necessary.

Asking Questions

In Section F on narrative inquiry, we pointed out that three elements of story were the *characters* in the story, the *setting* where the action of the story takes place, and the action itself, which unfolds over *time*. These elements prompt three questions that can be asked of the data—all in relation to the life experiences of the narrator. Although the three questions apply to narrative inquiry, they are equally important for all qualitative inquiry in which the focus of the exploration is the identity of the participants.

- *Who* is in the story and what happened or will happen *together*? The question asks about the characters in the story, their relationships and their positions vis-à-vis each other.
- *Where* does the action in the story take place, and what happened or will happen *there*? The question asks about the places and sequences of places where the story action takes place.
- *When* did or will the action in the story take place, and what happened or will happen *then*? The question asks about the time in which the action unfolds—past, present, and future.

Looking at the illustrative interview text (see Figure 4.2):

- Answers to the *who* question reveal the following characters in the story Alex tells: Alex the narrator and teacher educator; six different groups of his student teachers (line 2)
- Answers to the *where* question reveal: a master's program (line 1) at a university; his PhD program at his current university (lines 1 and 13)
- Answers to the *when* question reveal: when he started looking for a PhD program (line 1); three years after his master's (line 1); and now as a PhD student

From Implementation to Research

This is only a short piece of text, with few questions and answers, but we can see that if we make connections among the answers, we reach similar findings that we get from the exposure and reflection; that is, after three years of teaching a curriculum course to his student teachers, Alex realized that theoretically and pedagogically he was not delivering the type of course he wanted because of his own deficient knowledge in curriculum theory. He therefore decided to enroll in a university PhD program to develop himself professionally—and of interest to us, is the personal investment in his identity transformation.

Asking these questions systematically as you carefully read through the text requires you to examine it thoroughly, during which connections among the *who*, *where*, and *when* answers are made and become meaningful in relation to the topic or research questions of your research. To dig deeper into your topic, it is a good idea to follow each of the *who*, *where*, and *when* questions with a *why* question. Why do you get the answers you do? Why these answers and not other answers?

Searching for Themes

A thematic analysis involves searching the data for themes that are relevant to your research topic, that is, some identity-related topic. In the text, a behavior, an event, a thought, an opinion, a feeling, or an attitude could represent a theme. A *theme*, furthermore, is a conceptual representation of the actual life experience, so a theme is also often referred to as a *concept*.

The theme or concept will take the textual form of a word, a phrase, a sentence, or a group of sentences. So, from the illustrative interview text (see Figure 4.2), "I started to look for a PhD" is part of a sentence (= text form). On a conceptual level (= concept), it represents the theme of *future professional goal* (= theme).

The mechanics of thematic analysis involves reading the text or scanning the visual data in detail. When you have a lot of data, a useful way to manage the thematic analysis is through the process of *coding*, that is, assigning codes to the themes you discover during your analysis. Codes are names or tags (e.g., a word, color, letter, or number—something

259

From Implementation to Research

easy to remember) assigned to concepts that represent at a more abstract level the experiences, ideas, attitudes, or feelings identified in the data. In other words, the codes represent these concepts, which in turn represent the participant's identity experiences in the data.

After the data has been coded at this level, researchers can begin to examine collections of codes to see how they are related to each other. A set of codes denoting similar themes or concepts is grouped together to form a *category*, a higher level abstract concept. When you have a large amount of data, categorizing the themes in this way makes the data more manageable to work with, thereby assisting you to identify patterns within and between the different categories. Looking for relationships between and within categories is sometimes referred to as looking for patterns. *Patterns* are linkages at the conceptual level, so interpretation moves into an even higher gear during this stage.

In Alex's interview data (see Figure 4.2), we have identified four themes. Below we have indicated the relationship between a code, the theme or concept, and the associated text from the interview. We should caution at this point that you or someone else analyzing this interview (or any other data for that matter) may come up with a different set of themes. Coding for themes is not an exact science! And it does not necessarily have to be in exploratory action research because what is important is the process of exploring and observing action for you as the researcher to learn more about yourself and your own teaching context. The relevant text representing the theme in the extract is underlined and labelled A, B, C, or D in Figure 4.2.

A. goal (= code), *future professional goal* (= theme): This theme refers to the goal Alex set for himself, that is, finding an appropriate PhD program that would enable him to develop his knowledge so that he can address the shortcomings (theme D) in his knowledge and practice. In terms of identity, he realized (related to theme B) that his teacher educator identity needed changing in some way (i.e., further professional development to become a more informed, competent teacher educator).

From Implementation to Research

B. notice (= code), *new awareness or realization* (= theme): Repeated teaching of his curriculum module led to the realization that this module was deficient and that he needed to do something about it.

C. teach (= code), *teaching* (= theme): This theme refers to Alex's ownership of the curriculum module he teaches, the one with the problem.

D. problem (= code), *source of problem* (= theme): The specific problem is with the content of the module. This problem sparks the realization that he needs further professional development, so he begins his search for a PhD program.

This short illustrative text contains only one or two instances of each theme. Much larger sets of data will have many more, and it is then that coding and categorizing become particularly useful—coding to tag the themes so that they can be easily found in the data, and categorizing so that similar themes (there will be more when there is more data) can be combined to produce fewer categories that will then be easier to manage when seeking patterns of association among them and making interpretations in the process.

Content and Context

A final recommendation for researchers during the analysis stages of exploratory and action research is to 'lift your eyes' from your immediate situation or context and look beyond to wider contexts that interconnect with you and your work. So far in this section (Section G), the emphasis has been on the importance of understanding your own particular context during the analysis process, which is one of the central principles of exploratory action research. But looking beyond to wider contexts will add further meaning to your interpretations. It will enable you to make even more sense of who you are (your identity) in relation to your work or understand better who your learners or other research participants are as they negotiate their identities in their lives.

Figure 4.3 shows diagrammatically three *interrelated* levels of context expanding outwards.

261

From Implementation to Research

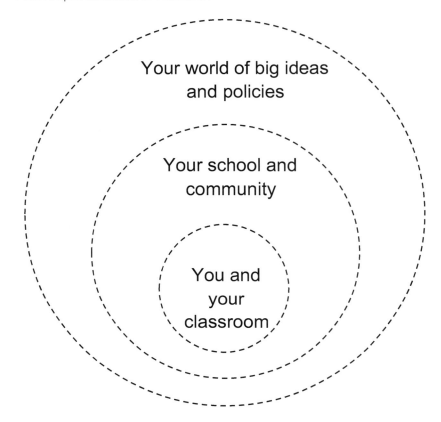

Figure 4.3 Expanding levels of context

- The inner, micro level represents you and your classroom. This is where you do your teaching and where you interact with your learners. Much exploratory action research focuses on what happens in this space.
- The middle level moves outward to focus on the school or institutional context in which you work and the community, meaning the people that are in some ways connected to the institution, including parents, recreational groups, community centers, medical and social work practitioners, city councils, and so on.
- The outer, macro level is the context often considered to be out of reach to most teachers, where teachers have less power to make decisions. But what happens at this level is very much connected to the work they do and hence connected to their identities. Examples

From Implementation to Research

of big ideas and decisions at this level include national language policies, external assessment regulations, new theories and developments in language learning and teacher education, large-scale curriculum transformation, state immigration policies, and even workload issues and pay scales! These all affect your work at the micro, classroom level.

In taking these levels of context into account during your data analysis — at every stage of the analysis — the following questions may guide you:

- How does this particular finding relate to what is happening at other contextual levels?
- With regard to this particular finding, would other teachers in the school find the same thing?
- Is my analysis being influenced by ideas beyond my control?
- How would this particular findings go down in the community of my learners?
- How does what I am finding now relate to my imagined identity in the future?

H. Sharing Your Findings

When you reach the end of the exploratory action research journey (see Section C and Figure 4.1), what happens next? Should you consider sharing the findings from your research? Some may argue that the point of the research was for *you* to learn more about *your* practice, *your* learners, *your* working conditions, and *your*self. Others may argue that sharing your research benefits others, too, because they will learn from what you have found. Also, sharing your research may give you a feeling of success, accomplishment, and ultimately empowerment.

Language teachers do share their research — more and more is there evidence of this. And the way they do so varies enormously. Here are some examples:

- having a conversation with a teacher colleague
- presenting a brief report at a school or departmental workshop or meeting

263

From Implementation to Research

- writing a book chapter (there are many opportunities opening up for teacher researchers)
- presenting a poster at a conference poster
- writing a short piece for professional association newsletters or journals
- contributing reports or commentaries or videos of your poster presentations to an association website; see, for example, the Research Special Interest Group (ReSIG) website of IATEFL (the International Association of Teachers of English as a Foreign Language): http://resig.weebly.com
- contributing to Facebook pages of associations and other professional groups; again, for example, IATEFL's ReSIG: www.facebook.com/groups/iateflresig
- engaging with and distributing your work on other social media, such as Twitter

In sharing your findings, it is vitally important to bear in mind the ethical implications of doing so. Your research may include information that participants do not want shared. Institutions may have their own regulations for conducting and sharing research, and it would be wise to consult them. In any case, you should ask yourself the following questions before sharing your findings — and it is always a good idea to consult with (more experienced) colleagues if you are not sure:

- Does my research include any photos or descriptions of children who cannot give consent to have their images or descriptions made public?
- Are there any participants from groups such as immigrants and refugees who might not want any or even some of their information shared?
- Is there any way the context of the study (e.g., school, institution, community) can be identified, and if so, might this be a problem?
- Have my participants told me any stories that were private?
- Should I go back to my participants and ask them if I can share their information in my report or presentation?
- How much of myself as researcher or teacher do I want to share? What might the consequences of the sharing be?

> **Further Reading**
>
> Curry, M. J., & Lillis, T. (Eds.). (2018). *Global academic publishing: Policies, perspectives and pedagogies*. Bristol: Multilingual Matters.
>
> ***Sample Study***
>
> Burns, A., & Westmacott, A. (2018). Teacher to researcher: Reflections on a new action research program for university EFL teachers. *Profile: Issues in Teachers' Professional Development*, *20*(1), 15–23.

I. Conclusion

Part 4 has brought to an end the research–practice–research cycle that forms the organizational structure of this book. The book started with the research of others and ended with a focus on conducting your own research. In between, the practical implementations consisting of the activities in Part 2 and the suggestions for actually using them in Part 3, reflected the outcomes of the former research and prompted the latter recommended procedures for exploratory action research. The aim throughout has been to offer you, your learners, and by extension through the sharing of your research findings, your colleagues, the opportunity to reflect on and communicate your identities and possibly transform them in the process.

References

Aaker, J. (1997). Dimensions of brand personality. *Journal of Marketing Research*, *34*, 347–356.

Al-Qahtani, Z., & Al Zumor, A. W. (2016). Saudi parents' attitudes towards using English as a medium of instruction in private primary schools. *International Journal of Applied Linguistics and English Literature*, *5*(1), 18–32.

Barcelos, A. M. F. (2015). Unveiling the relationship between language learning beliefs, emotions, and identities. *Studies in Second Language Learning and Teaching*, *5*(2), 301–325.

Barkhuizen, G. (Ed.). (2017). *Reflections on language teacher identity research*. New York, NY: Routledge.

Barkhuizen, G. (Ed.). (2019). *Qualitative research topics in language teacher education*. New York, NY: Routledge.

Barkhuizen, G., Benson, P., & Chik, A. (2014). *Narrative inquiry in language teaching and learning research*. New York, NY: Routledge.

Beauchamp, C., & Thomas, L. (2009). Understanding teacher identity: An overview of issues in the literature and implications for teacher education. *Cambridge Journal of Education*, *39*(2), 175–189.

Benson, P., Barkhuizen, G., Bodycott, P., & Brown, J. (2013). *Second language identity in narratives of study abroad*. London: Palgrave Macmillan.

Block, D. (2007). *Second language identities*. London: Continuum.

Blommaert, J. (2006). Language policy and national identity. In T. Ricento (Ed.), *Language policy: Theory and method* (pp. 238–254). Oxford: Blackwell.

Borg, S. (2013). *Teacher research in language teaching: A critical analysis*. Cambridge: Cambridge University Press.

Bourdieu, P. (1977). The economics of linguistic exchanges. *Social Science Information*, *16*(6), 645–668.

Bucholtz, M. (2003). Sociolinguistic nostalgia and authentication of identity. *Journal of Sociolinguistics*, *7*(3), 398–416.

Burns, A., & Westmacott, A. (2018). Teacher to researcher: Reflections on a new action research program for university EFL teachers. *Profile: Issues in Teachers' Professional Development*, *20*(1), 15–23.

Chapman, G., & Beagan, B. (2013). Food practices and transnational identities. *Food, Culture & Society*, *16*, 367–386.

Curry, M. J., & Lillis, T. (Eds.). (2018). *Global academic publishing: Policies, perspectives and pedagogies*. Bristol: Multilingual Matters.

Darvin, R., & Norton, B. (2015). Identity and a model of investment in applied linguistics. *Annual Review of Applied Linguistics*, *35*, 36–56.

De Bono, E. (1982). *De Bono's thinking course*. Chatham: BBC Books.

References

De Costa, P. I., & Norton, B. (2016). Identity in language learning and teaching: Research agendas for the future. In S. Preece (Ed.), *Routledge handbook of language and identity* (pp. 586–601). Abingdon: Routledge.

Dikilitaş, K., & Hanks, J. (Eds.). (2018). *Developing language teachers with exploratory practice: Innovations and explorations in language education*. Basingstoke: Palgrave Macmillan.

Dikilitaş, K., & Yaylı, D. (2018). Teachers' professional identity development through action research. *English Language Teaching Journal, 72*(4), 415–424.

Douglas Fir Group. (2016). A transdisciplinary framework for SLA in a multilingual world. *The Modern Language Journal, 100*(S), 19–47.

Duncan, I. (2001). The pros and cons of cages. *Worlds Poultry Science Journal, 57*, 389–390.

Edwards, R. (2015). Software and the hidden curriculum in digital education. *Pedagogy, Culture and Society, 23*, 265–279.

Farrell, T. S. C. (2015). *Promoting teacher reflection in second language education: A framework for TESOL professionals*. New York, NY: Routledge.

Ford, K. (2016). The taped monologue as narrative technique for reflective practice. *English Language Teaching Journal, 70*(3), 253–260.

Gay, G. (2000). *Culturally responsive teaching: Theory, research, and practice*. New York, NY: Teachers College Press.

Gee, J. P. (1990). *Social linguistics and literacies: Ideology in discourses*. London: Falmer.

Gee, J. P. (2000). Identity as an analytic lens for research in education. *Review of Research in Education, 25*, 99–125.

Graves, K. (2001). A framework of course development processes. In D. Hall & A. Hewings (Eds.), *Innovation in English language teaching: A reader* (pp. 178–196). London: Open University Press.

Graves, K. (2008). The language curriculum: A social contextual perspective. *Language Teaching, 41*(2), 147–181.

Hadfield, J. (2018). Covert syllabuses. *Folio, 18*(2), 25–29.

Harison, R. (2008). *"It's my think": Exploring critical literacy with low level EAL students* (Unpublished master's dissertation). Auckland University of Technology, Auckland.

Harré, R. (2001). Metaphysics and narrative. In J. Brockmeier & D. Carbaugh (Eds.), *Narrative and identity: Studies in autobiography, self and culture* (pp. 59–73). Amsterdam: John Benjamins.

Ivanič, R. (2006). Language, learning and identification. In R. Kiely, P. Rea-Dickins, H. Woodfield, & G. Clibbon (Eds.), *Language, culture and identity in applied linguistics* (pp. 7–29). London: Equinox.

Johnson, K., & Golombek, P. (Eds.). (2002). *Teachers' narrative inquiry as professional development*. Cambridge: Cambridge University Press.

Jones, R. H., & Richards, J. C. (Eds.). (2016). *Creativity in language teaching: Perspectives from research and practice*. New York, NY: Routledge.

Kanno, Y., & Norton, B. (2003). Imagined communities and educational possibilities: Introduction. *Journal of Language, Identity, and Education, 2*(4), 241–249.

Koo, Y. L. (2009). Mobilising learners through English as Lingua Franca (ELF): Providing access to culturally diverse international learners in higher education.

References

In P. Kell & G. Vogl (Eds.), *Global student mobility in the Asia Pacific: Mobility, migration, security and wellbeing of international students* (pp. 74–87). Newcastle Upon Tyne: Cambridge Scholars Publishing.

Kramsch, C. (1993). *Context and culture in language teaching*. Oxford: Oxford University Press.

Markus, H., & Nurius, P. (1986). Possible selves. *American Psychologist*, *41*, 954–969.

Nero, S. (2005). Language, identities and ESL pedagogy. *Language and Education*, *19*(3), 194–211.

Norton, B. (1995). Social identity, investment, and language learning. *TESOL Quarterly*, *29*(1), 9–31.

Norton, B. (1997). Language, identity, and the ownership of English. *TESOL Quarterly*, *31*(3), 409–429.

Norton, B. (2013). *Identity and language learning: Extending the conversation* (2nd ed.). Bristol: Multilingual Matters.

Norton, B. (2015). Identity, investment, and faces of English internationally. *Chinese Journal of Applied Linguistics*, *38*(4), 375–391.

Ochs, E., & Capps, L. (2001). *Living narrative*. London: Harvard University Press.

Pavlenko, A., & Blackledge, A. (2004). Introduction: New theoretical approaches to the study of negotiation of identities in multilingual contexts. In A. Pavlenko & A. Blackledge (Eds.), *Negotiation of identities in multilingual contexts* (pp. 1–33). Clevedon: Multilingual Matters.

Pavlenko, A., & Norton, B. (2007). Imagined communities, identity, and English language teaching. In J. Cummins & C. Davison (Eds.), *International handbook of English language teaching* (pp. 669–680). New York, NY: Springer.

Smith, R., & Rebolledo, P. (2018). *A handbook for exploratory action research*. British Council. Retrieved March 10, 2019, from https://englishagenda. britishcouncil.org/sites/default/files/attachments/30510_bc_explore_ actions_handbook_online_aw.pdf

Soh, K. (2017). Fostering student creativity through teacher behaviors. *Thinking Skills and Creativity*, *23*, 58–66.

Sung, C. C. M. (2019). Investments and identities across contexts: A case study of a Hong Kong undergraduate student's L2 learning experiences. *Journal of Language, Identity and Education*, *18*(3), 190–203.

Tin, T. B. (2013). Towards creativity in ELT: The need to say something new. *English Language Teaching Journal*, *67*(4), 385–397.

Tracy, K., & Robles, J. S. (2013). *Everyday talk: Building and reflecting identities*. New York, NY: Guilford Press.

Varghese, M., Morgan, B., Johnston, B., & Johnson, K. A. (2005). Theorizing language teacher identity: Three perspectives and beyond. *Journal of Language, Identity, and Education*, *4*(1), 21–44.

Wette, R. (2009). Making the instructional curriculum as an interactive, contextualized process: Case studies of seven ESOL teachers. *Language Teaching Research*, *13*(4), 337–365.

Wette, R. (2010). Product-process distinctions in ELT curriculum theory and practice. *English Language Teaching Journal*, *65*(2), 136–144.

Wyatt, M., & Márquez, C. P. (2016). Helping first-year undergraduates engage in language research. *Language Teaching Research*, *20*(2), 146–164.

Yim, S. Y. (2016). EFL young learners: Their imagined communities and language learning. *English Language Teaching Journal*, *70*(1), 57–65.

Ylimaki, R. (2013). Create a comprehensive, rigorous, and coherent curricular program. In R. Ylimaki (Ed.), *The new instructional leadership ISLLC standard two* (pp. 45–60). New York, NY: Routledge.

Index

Note: Page numbers in *italics* indicate figures; page numbers in **bold** indicate tables.

activities: flexibility in adapting 29–30; implementing in classroom 225–234; learners interacting 1–2; organization of 26–30; teachers planning 223–225; titles and aims for imagining identities **173–175**; titles and aims for projecting identities **79–82**; titles and aims for recognizing identities **125–128**; titles and aims for reflexing identities **30–32**

advertising *see* Language of Ads; Social Justice and Advertising

Aliens Have Landed: activity of imagining identities **173**, 189–192; extension for 192; language practice 189; procedure for 190–192; teacher reflection for 192

Ambedkar, B.R. 198

animal *see* What Kind of Wild Animal?

Arabic language 224

Auckland Museum, New Zealand 122, 123

Author Presence: activity for reflexing identities **32**, 66–69; extension for 69; language practice 67; procedure for 67–69; teacher reflection for 69

Barkhuizen, Gary 7

Being Chinese in Aoteoroa (exhibition) 122, 123

Brault, Robert 198

cartoon *see* Make Your Own Cartoon

Celebrating Birthdays: activity for reflexing identities **30**, 35–38; extension for 37; language practice 36; procedure for 36–37; teacher reflection for 37; worksheet for 38

Chbosky, Stephen 198

Chickens in Cages: activity for reflexing identities **32**, 70–74; extension for 71–72; formal and informal language 74; implementing 227, 228, 232; language practice 70; procedure for 71; teacher reflection for 72; worksheet for 72–74

Clarke, John Henrik 197

classroom life: engaging classification 244; manageable classification 243; reflection on 242–243; significant classification 243–244; urgent classification 243

Clothes We Wear: activity of projecting identities **80**, 95–98; language practice 96; procedure for 96–98; teacher reflection for 98

communicating identities 2, 228; imagining identities 24; projecting identities 23; recognizing identities 23; reflexing identities 22–23

Consumer Identity: activity of imagining identities **175**, 208–213; extension for 210; group work 211–212; individual work 212–213; language practice 209; procedure

270

Index

for 209–210; teacher reflection for 211; worksheets for 211–213

creativity 219, 235, 236

curriculum 219; characteristics of 220–222; dimensions of 220; enactment 234; hidden 220, 221; instructional 220; planned 220–221

data collection, exploratory action research 248–252

day-to-day social interaction 13–14

De Costa, Peter 2

Designing a Questionnaire: activity of recognizing identities **127**, 156–160; implementing 234; language practice 156; materials for 158–160; procedure for 156–158; teacher reflection for 158; variation for 158

Different Perspectives: activity of imagining identities **174**, 199–202; extension for 200–201; implementing 229; language practice 199; procedure for 200; teacher reflection for 201; worksheet for 202

digital literacy 5, 237

discourses 13

dream room *see* My Dream Room

Dr. Seuss 197, 198

English: importance of learning 224; *see also* Speaking English Tomorrow

essentialism 8–9

ethnic identity 24

exploratory action research 237; analyzing information gathered 254–263; asking questions 258–259; classifying as manageable, urgent, significant and engaging (MUSE) 243–244; critical reflection of data 256–258; determining content and context 261–263; expanding levels of

context *262*; The Genders of Objects 245; A Good Friend 244–245; information gathering for 248–252; interview extract *256*; multiple exposure to data 256–258; narrative inquiry as approach 252–254; post-activity teacher reflections 245–247; reflecting on classroom life 242–243; searching for themes in 259–261; selecting topics for 242–248; sharing findings of 263–264; steps in 239, 240, *241*; suggestions for topic resources 247–248

Facebook 225, 264; *see also* Why is Facebook so Popular?

Film Critic: activity of recognizing identities **125**, 134–138; extension for 137; language practice 135; procedure for 136; teacher reflection for 137; worksheet for 137

Food and Identity: activity of reflexing identities **32**, 61–66; extension for 64; language practice 61; procedure for 62–64; teacher reflection for 65; worksheet for 65–66

gamers *see* Names for (Online) Gamers

Gates, Bill 112

Gay Men Playing Rugby: activity of projecting identities **80**, 90–92; language practice 91; procedure for 91–92; teacher reflection for 92

gender identity 24

Gendered Identities in Occupations: activity of recognizing identities **126**, 145–148; language practice 146; procedures for 146–147; teacher reflection for 147

Genders of Objects: activity of reflexing identities **32**, 58–61; language practice 59; procedure

271

Index

for 59–60; research topics arising from 245; task sheets 61; teacher reflection for 60

globalization 3–4, 237

Good Friend: activity of recognizing identities **125**, 128–131; extension for 130; language practice 129; procedure for 129–130; research topics arising from 244; teacher reflection for 130–131

Gruwell, Erin 197

hidden syllabus 222

holiday *see* My Ideal Holiday

IATEFL Research Special Interest Group 101, 263–264

identity: application implications 21–25; definition of 14; research on 2; term 7–8; term subject positions over 10; *see also* communicating identity; language learner identity; language teacher identity

Identity Quotes: activity of imagining identities **174**, 195–199; extension for 196–197; language practice 195; procedure for 195–196; teacher reflection for 197; worksheet for 197–199

Identity Theft: activity of recognizing identities **126**, 138–141; language practice 139; procedure for 139–140; teacher reflection for 140–141

Idiomatic Language: activity of projecting identities **81**, 103–106; extension/variation for 105; language practice 103–104; planning 223–225; procedure for 104–105; teacher reflection for 105; worksheet for 105–106

imagining identities 24, 246; activity titles and aims **173–175**; organization of activities 26–30;

research implications and activities **27**

imagining identities activities: The Aliens Have Landed **173**, 189–192; Consumer Identity **175**, 208–213; Different Perspectives **174**, 199–202; Identity Quotes **174**, 195–199; Me Flying High **173**, 178–181; My Dream Room **173**, 182–185; Names for (Online) Gamers **173**, 185–189; Social Justice and Advertising **175**, 205–208; Speaking English Tomorrow **174**, 192–195; Transport of the Future **175**, 213–218; What Kind of Wild Animal? **173**, 175–178; What Makes Them Them? **174**, 202–205

immigrant(s) as language learners 10–11

Immigration Museum, Melbourne, Australia 123

inequality of people, groups and institutions 12

information gathering: asking questions of 258–259; content and context of 261–263; exploratory action research 248–252; making sense of 254–263; multiple exposure and critical reflection of 256–258; searching for themes in 259–261; *see also* exploratory action research

intersectionality 4–5

Introducing Ourselves: activity of projecting identities **79**, 82–86; extension for 85; language practice 83; listening task sheet 86; procedure for 83–85; teacher reflection for 85

investment 4

Justifying Your Opinion: activity of projecting identities **82**, 119–122;

Index

implementing 228, 232; language practice 120; procedure for 120–121; teacher reflection for 121–122; variation for 121

Kalam, A.P.J. Abdul 197

language learner identity: conceptualizing 7–16, 21; construction across time and space 9–10; day-to-day social interaction 13–14; giving learners opportunity to speak 15–16; inequitable social structures of 11–12; language as constitutive of and constituted by 14–15; possibilities for the future 10–11; relationship to world 8–9
language learning 1; discourse 13; research agenda issues 3–7
Language of Ads: activity of recognizing identities **128**, 169–173; extension for 171; implementing 229; language practice 169; procedure for 170–171; teacher reflection for 171–172; worksheet for 173
language teacher identity 1, 3: conceptualizing 16–21; struggle and harmony in negotiation of 18, 19–20
language teaching: discourse 13; research agenda issues 3–7

Make Your Own Cartoon: activity of projecting identities **81**, 106–111; extension for 110; implementing 227; language practice 108; procedure for 108–110; teacher reflection for 110–111
Maps of the World: activity for reflexing identities **31**, 49–53; extension/ variation for 51; implementing 228, 232; language practice 50; procedure for 50–51; teacher reflection for 51; worksheet for 52–53

Me Flying High: activity of imagining identities **173**, 178–181; extension for 180; language practice 179; procedure for 179–180; teacher reflection for 180–181
Memories and Smells: activity for reflexing identities **31**, 46–49; extension/variation for 48–49; implementing 230; language practice 47; procedure for 47–48; teacher reflection for 49
migrant identity 24
Migration Museum, London 123
Montessori, Maria 197
My Dream Room: activity of imagining identities **173**, 182–185; extension for 184; language practice 182; procedure for 182–183; teacher reflection for 184; worksheet for 185
My Ideal Holiday: activity for reflexing identities **32**, 75–79; categories of tourists 78; extension for 77; language practice 75; procedure for 76–77; teacher reflection for 77; worksheet for 78–79

Names for (Online) Gamers: activity of imagining identities **173**, 185–189; extension for 187–188; implementing 227, 231; language practice 185; procedure for 186–187; teacher reflection for 188; worksheets for 188–189
narrative inquiry 238; collecting and analyzing stories 253; constructing stories from data 254; exploratory action research 252–254
national identity 24; *see also* Questioning National Identities
No Laughing Matter: activity of recognizing identities **127**, 165–169; extension for 168; implementing 229; language practice 166;

273

Index

procedure for 167–168; teacher reflection for 169
Norman, Donald 197
Norton, Bonny 1, 2, 7

perspective, poststructuralist 10; *see also* Different Perspectives
Pictures at an Exhibition: activity of projecting identities **82**, 122–124; extension for 124; language practice 123; procedure for 123–124; teacher reflection for 124
projecting identities 23, 244, 246; activity titles and aims **79–82**; organization of activities 26–30; research implications and activities **27**
projecting identities activities: The Clothes We Wear **80**, 95–98; Gay Men Playing Rugby **80**, 90–93; Idiomatic Language **81**, 103–106; Introducing Ourselves **79**, 82–86; Justifying Your Opinion **82**, 119–122; Make Your Own Cartoon **81**, 106–111; Pictures at an Exhibition **82**, 122–125; Proverbs and You **81**, 114–119; Relationships and Age **80**, 93–95; There's a Little Bit of Good in Everyone **81**, 111–121; What's in a Name? **79**, 86–90; Why is Facebook so Popular? **80**, 98–103
Proverbs and You: activity of projecting identities **81**, 114–119; extension for 116; group work for 117–118; individual work for 118–119; language practice 115; procedure for 115–116; teacher reflection for 116–117

qualitative research topics 247–248
Questioning National Identities: activity of recognizing identities **127**, 151–155; extension/variation

for 154; implementing 230, 231; language practice 152; procedure for 152–154; teacher reflection for 155
questionnaire *see* Designing a Questionnaire
quotes *see* Identity Quotes
Quran 224

racial identity 24
recognizing identities 23, 244, 246; activity titles and aims **125–128**; organization of activities 26–30; research implications and activities **27**
recognizing identities activities: Designing a Questionnaire **127**, 156–160; Film Critic **125**, 134–138; Gendered Identities in Occupations **126**, 145–148; A Good Friend **125**, 128–131; Identity Theft **126**, 138–141; The Language of Ads **128**, 165–173; No Laughing Matter **127**, 165–170; Questioning National Identities **127**, 151–156; Stereotyping **126**, 148–151; Teacher Roles **126**, 141–145; Who Are These Women? **125**, 131–134; Writing a Report **127**, 160–165
reflexing identities 22–23, 226, 245; activity titles and aims **30–32**; organization of activities 26–30; research implications and activities **27**
reflexing identities activities: Author Presence **32**, 66–69; Celebrating Birthdays **30**, 35–39; Chickens in Cages **32**, 70–74; Food and Identity **32**, 61–66; The Genders of Objects **32**, 58–61; Maps of the World **31**, 49–53; Memories and Smells **31**, 46–49; My Ideal Holiday **32**, 75–79; This Is (Not) Like Me **30**, 33–35; Tweeting **31**, 42–46; Using Our

Index

Brains! **31**, 53–58; What Makes Me Me? **31**, 38–41

Relationships and Age: activity of projecting identities **80**, 93–95; language practice 93; procedure for 93–95; teacher reflection for 95

research agenda: communicating identity 22–25; digital literacy 5; globalization 3–4; intersectionality 4–5; investment 4; scales 6; social theory across disciplines 5; teacher identities 6–7; *see also* exploratory action research

scales 6, 12

second language acquisition (SLA) 7, 13

Shaw, George Bernard 198

Shutterstock 180

social class identity 25

Social Justice and Advertising: activity of imagining identities **175**, 205–208; extension for 207; implementing 227, 229; language practice 205; procedure for 206–207; teacher reflection for 207; worksheet for 207–208

social media 264; *see also* Why is Facebook so Popular?

social structures 8, 11–12

social theory 5

Speaking English Tomorrow: activity of imagining identities **174**, 192–195; language practice 193; narrative frame for 194; procedure for 193–194; teacher reflection for 194, 246–247

Stereotyping: activity of recognizing identities **127**, 148–151; extension for 150; implementing 230; language practice 149; procedure for 149–150; teacher reflection for 150, 246; worksheet for 151

teacher(s): creativity of 219, 235, 236; identities 1, 3; language 1; planning

activities 223–225; research agenda on 6–7

Teacher Roles: activity of recognizing identities **126**, 141–145; extension for 144; implementing 232; language practice 142; procedure for 142–144; teacher reflection for 144–145; worksheet for 145

technology, digital literacy 5

TESOLANZ, New Zealand 101

There's a Little Bit of Good in Everyone: activity of projecting identities **81**, 111–121; extension for 113; procedure for 112–113; teacher reflection for 113; worksheets for 113–121

This Is (Not) Like Me: activity for reflexing identities **30**, 33–35; implementing 226; language practice 33; procedure for 34–35; teacher reflection for 35

Toth, K.L. 198

Transport of the Future: activity of imagining identities **175**, 213–218; implementing 228; language practice 214; materials for 215–217; procedure for 214–215; teacher reflection for 215; worksheet for 217–218

Tweeting: activity for reflexing identities **31**, 42–46; implementing 227, 231; language practice 42; procedure for 43–44; teacher reflection for 44; worksheet for 44–46

Using Our Brains!: activity for reflexing identities **31**, 53–58; extension for 55; implementing 227, 229; language practice 54; materials for 56–57; procedure for 54–56; teacher reflection for 55–56; worksheet for 57–58

What Kind of Wild Animal?: activity of imagining identities **173**, 175–178;

275

Index

extension for 177; implementing 227; language practice 176; procedure for 176–177; teacher reflection for 178

What Makes Me Me?: activity for reflexing identities **31**, 38–41; extension for 41; implementing 202, 226, 231, 233; language practice 39; procedure for 40–41; teacher reflection for 41

What Makes Them Them?: activity of imagining identities **174**, 202–205; implementing 231; language practice 203; procedure for 203–204; teacher reflection for 204

What's in a Name?: activity of projecting identities **79**, 86–90; extension/variation for 88; implementing 228; language practice 87; procedure for 87–88; teacher reflection for 89; worksheets for 89–90

Who Are These Women?: activity of recognizing identities **125**, 131–134; extension for 133; language practice 132; procedure for 132–133; teacher reflection for 134

Why is Facebook so Popular?: activity of projecting identities **80**, 98–103; extension for 100–101; implementing 227, 231; procedure for 99–100; teacher reflection for 101; worksheet for 101–103

women *see* Who Are These Women?

Writing a Report: activity of recognizing identities **127**, 160–165; implementing 226, 232, 234; language practice 161; materials for 163–165; procedure for 161–162; teacher reflection for 162–163